EMAIL IS NOT DEAD

How To Stop Losing Customers, Find Hidden Profit, And Turn One-Off Sales Into Lifetime ROI

Karly McFarland

Print ISBN: 978-1-7782438-0-6

Edited by Sky Nuttall
Cover Design by Andrea Huerta
Layout by Hynek Palatin

Disclaimer
The information in this book was deemed to be correct at the time of publication, but the author does not assume any liability for loss or damage caused by errors or omissions. The publisher and author are not responsible for any actions you take or do not take as a result of reading this book, and are not liable for any damages or negative consequences from action or inaction of any person reading or following the information in this book. Readers are aware that the websites referenced are subject to change or become obsolete. The materials in this book are for informational purposes only and not for the purpose of providing legal advice. You should contact your legal counsel to obtain advice with respect to any particular questions or concerns.

Contents

Foreword

By Jake Cohen, VP of Content at Klaviyo

Email is a balding, middle aged retiree-in-waiting.

The first email was sent in 1971, which makes the protocol 51 years old. It might be old, but it isn't dead.

And in truth, email may be more akin to salt than an aging human. Salt – yes, that stuff in the ocean and on the dinner table – has been an exceptionally important part of society for thousands of years. In ancient antiquity, salt was the currency civilizations used to exchange value; people literally traded salt for food. As time has passed, the way salt is used and valued has certainly changed – now you get it for free in your takeout order. But it has never gone away.

Email, too, has undergone quite the metamorphosis. It started as an electronic message sent between computers within the same network within the same building and now there are 333 billion emails sent to people all around the world every day. And along the way, the secret keepers of the sanctity of email have had to protect the sacred channel from the human condition.

The first spam email was sent in 1978 – Gary, a marketer at ARPANET (go figure), was trying to sell off some extra servers he shouldn't have bought. Over the past 40+ years, thousands of people have dedicated their lives to keep the Gary's of the world from polluting our inboxes. This isn't to say it's always been smooth sailing. Nigerian princes and doctors selling Viagra seem to have been the most common senders in the 1990s – fortunately, we've come a long way since then.

This cat and mouse chase that has evolved the inbox filtering community has presented material challenges for marketers who are sending useful information to people who genuinely want it. And if getting through spam filters wasn't enough, the increasing competition for human attention has put tremendous pressure on marketers to make and design emails that are memorable and inspire people to act, not just see.

But because of these valiant efforts to protect our inboxes, email thrives. It's how we receive birthday invitations. It's how we share quarterly updates. It's how we plan trips, reminisce on the good ol' days and confirm a Venmo payment was sent. Email is how we communicate and connect.

For marketers, email is one of the best ways to connect with your customers and, yes, make money. But as powerful as email can be, use it wrong and it will wrong you.

I've personally spent years learning the ins and outs of spam filters, effective design, deliverability infrastructure, revenue-generating email strategy, the secrets of list building and how to not piss off the Gmail underlords. I can tell you – it's all addressed here.

Every once in a while you get the serendipity of picking something up that seems interesting and turns out to be wildly useful. *Email Is Not Dead* is one of those books. Soak it in and enjoy.

Preface

Why

Email marketing saved my life.

I know, I know ... you might think I'm being hyperbolic, but it's the truth. While this is a technical book packed with everything you must know about leveraging the most powerful growth and retention channel on the planet—my story is quietly woven into each insight.

Today, I'm known as the (recovering) workaholic CEO of a rapidly growing 7-figure marketing agency that's worked with hundreds of eCommerce clients.

But getting here was a rollercoaster.

I need to take you back because it'll show you how invested I am in your success. No matter how "crazy" or radical your goals are, I'm here to ride shotgun with you and make them real.

Growing up, I was endlessly fascinated with learning—about everything. A spirit fueled by a sense of wonder, possibility, and curiosity. A kid with a wide-eyed imagination.

Until I wasn't.

There's no faster way to kill that spirit than by moving 50+ times before the ripe age of 20. Forget money; I had no stable ground. Each day was a mystery of where I'd lay my head at night.

So, what did I do? Well, much like you reading this book, I controlled what I could—my work ethic. When you've got no control of a chaotic life, there are two options: give in or become the most hard-working, determined—and above all—the toughest person around.

This can-do attitude worked.

I became an achievement machine, including a college-level reading comprehension level at age 9, grading in the 99th percentile for the entire state of California in every state-wide exam, a 4.3 high school GPA, and a mile-long list of accolades.

I don't mean this to brag, but they're genuinely endless. Some neuroses? Probably. A dash of unhealthy competition? You got me. (I'm still pissed I got a B, *a freaking B* in high school Spanish.)

But I share this with you because my grit and determination make me great at what I do, but most importantly, it means I care.

September 10th, 2013

"Your mom didn't come home today," her boyfriend says to me after I open the sliding door and step into our double-wide trailer.

The tension is palpable, but I'm too tired to care. I'd finished an 8-hour shift after a morning packed with classes, and now it was time to set dinner. Remember what I said about being an overachiever?

"Nothing new," I thought as I slacked off my faded orange backpack and put dinner on the table.

Days go by, and she's still not home.

Now things are getting weird. *Uncomfortable.* This on-again, off-again boyfriend had kicked me out before—the first time at age 12. He was pissed at my mom but took it out on me. I'd done nothing wrong.

And now that anger was back.

We called jails, hospitals, and her friends. She was nowhere to be found. A week after she went missing, I got a call from my aunt, "I spoke to your mom. She isn't coming home. She's starting a new life."

Thanks for the update, Mom.

My world was crumbling. The fact my mom wasn't coming back meant that I was no longer welcome in my home. I needed to grow up and "get at it," as my grandpa always said.

What did that look like? I needed to find a better-paying job and provide for myself. I had no idea what I would do. But I did the only thing I knew—execute. I hustled. And I found a great job that was two hours away.

With a trash bag full of clothes and a broken dream, I dropped out of university and found a place to live. The tiny house was $500 a month for rent—what a score! But that Walmart price tag came with boarded-up windows and zero ventilation. Taking a shower meant watching (and hearing) the *drip, drip, drip* of the water from the ceilings.

Classy.

I had nothing. A few belongings. No money. What I did have and what you, as an entrepreneur reading this book, have is unique. It's a special sauce. It makes you unlike others. And it's why you choose to carve your own path.

All I had was sheer determination to survive. And survive, I did.

After a while, though, survival gets old. Sure, desperation creates a level of urgency that propels you. But as time passes ... you know that you're meant for more.

Two years later, I was still trying to figure it out ...

CHECKING SUMMARY	Chase College Checking	
		AMOUNT
Beginning Balance		$1,377.14
Deposits and Additions		1,093 90
ATM & Debit Card Withdrawals		- 1,560 16
Electronic Withdrawals		- 111 99
Ending Balance		$798.89

I had no money, but that sure as hell didn't mean I acted like it.

I could see a future beyond my current circumstances and would not let my sobering reality stop me. This is what makes us special, right? While most people get anchored by today's circumstances, we envision a better future.

Even when it doesn't make sense.

As far as my job? Crushed it. Just like in school. But it was different now. I was a grown adult that had zero purpose. No sense of direction in life. And no family.

But I had a ridiculous and insatiable personal drive, a stubborn sense of agency that acted as a motivating force.

A couple of years later, it started to click.

I found myself working online for a Santa Monica-based company. It led to seeing my dream unfold in real-time. Entrepreneurship was the vehicle to make one's dreams come true. Finally, I could control my destiny and not rely on others.

Working with someone who'd been part of Elon Musk's inner circle at Tesla not only showed me what was possible—it blew my world *wide-freaking-open*.

By harnessing the time-tested principles of influence with the most reliable (and potent) growth and retention tool on the planet, email marketing …

We could create money out of thin air. We could compel people to act. We could build a tribe of raving fans who not only wanted what we had to offer but paid us with a smile.

Just. Using. Email.

Whoa, mind blown. I continued to check off boxes that I only had in my wildest of dreams. I was able to work remotely. Set my schedule. Move to another country with my friends and finally, *finally*, find a sense of stability.

Then, at a random co-working space in Medellin, Colombia, I met the future co-founder of my agency. A few months later, we planted a seed. We set a lofty (what 99% would call delusional) goal at the time:

We were going to make $100,000 a month.

Turning a one-off freelance income into a 7-figure agency isn't a cakewalk. Thousands have failed. But we saw an opportunity. We used what all those valleys provided me with—a relentless work ethic and unlimited grit.

I fell head over heels with marketing. Specifically, email marketing captured my heart. Something about the ability to create opportunities on demand, connect deeply with customers, and cultivate long-term value.

In the first three months, we had 10X'd revenue. In roughly two years, we grew to a 7-figure agency that would work with brands on Shark Tank, several of Tai Lopez's household brands, plus become a top Klaviyo partner. Winning.

Best of all, we helped transform the businesses (and lives) of over 500+ entrepreneurs. Every step of the way, I poured my heart and soul into the craft. I met many business owners stuck in the gap of what their business and life could be ... but there was a chasm in the way.

Using email marketing, I was able to help them work towards eliminating that chasm. Today, you'll hear this everywhere, "Email marketing is dead."

And they're right. It's dead if you have no strategy, no automation, and use it as a firehose to blast your subscribers. But for the 1% of businesses who use it strategically ...

It's a competitive advantage to stop losing customers, find hidden profits, and turn one-off sales into a lifetime of ROI. And I want you to be next.

So, back to that opening line: email marketing did save my life. My chaotic childhood gave me a superpower—I help businesses of all sizes create stability, predictability, and freedom.

While your stakes may not be as dramatic, they're as important.

If you're here, there's a problem you need to fix. What worked a few years ago isn't working now. You're losing market share to competitors. Churn is costing you dearly. You've got a stellar brand that people love … but they're not coming back for more. And it's costing you more than just cash.

I'm here to fix that.

As you can tell, I'll go to the ends of the earth with you to make it happen.

Because let's be real: there's a lot of noise and so-called "gurus" in the marketing world. So let me be direct and tell you why you should listen to me.

For starters, if you made it this far…you either think I'm crazy or obsessed. You're right, and the years I've invested in discovering and applying the strategies in this book are now yours.

Second, everything I teach is 100% rooted in tangible metrics, data and results —because theories don't generate results. Trust me, I was tired of the fluff out there, too.

Lastly, while I believe this is the guide to transforming your business, I'm humble enough to recognize there's so much more to learn. I don't know about you, but I want the people I learn from always to push themselves to grow, expand and stay ahead of ever-changing trends.

On the surface, this book is about email marketing, but it's really about so much more. It's the culmination of my life's work. And for you, certainly, this book is about your potential as a marketer, a business owner—and the specific actions you can take to turn your dreams into a reality.

There is no other guide like this on the planet. Trust me, I looked. It doesn't exist. All I found were fluff marketing books or glorified blog posts as chapters with minimal tangible, actionable advice.

So I wrote it. I've done the hardest part for you. All I need is for you to meet me halfway and take action.

The rest? Well, that'll be your story to tell.

CHAPTER 1

Deliverability

Words to Know

IP ADDRESS: An IP address is represented by a unique string of numbers that indicates where a message is being sent from. In the past, an IP address was the prime form of sender identification.

Unfortunately, many spammers have taken advantage of this system by filtering through IP addresses to suit their needs. Because of this, mailbox providers now look at the domain equally to identify an email's sender.

IP POOL: An IP Pool is a group (pool) of senders (brands) utilizing the same IP. ESPs put senders on a shared IP by default, as 99.9% of senders are best suited for this type of setup. An IP Pool allows senders to leverage each other's sending practices to maintain good standing.

DEDICATED IP: A dedicated IP hosts only a single sender. This sender is completely self-reliant on their own sending practices to maintain good standing. Dedicated

IPs are generally utilized by brands with a very high volume of emails and a deliverability specialist on staff.

SENDING DOMAIN: Sending domain is a recognizable form of sender identification. A sender's domain is listed after the @ symbol in their email address. This indicates to subscribers and mailbox providers where the message came from—and unlike IP addresses, domains are a bit harder to dispose of. For example, my email address karly@emailisnotdead.co shows ISPs that I'm on the emailisnotdead.co domain.

SENDING REPUTATION: Sending reputation takes into account the sending history of an IP address. Just as credit card companies will look at your credit score to see how much they can trust you, mailbox providers look at sending history for the same reason. A lack of sending history doesn't allow mailbox providers to determine if an email belongs in the inbox or spam folder, so they place additional restrictions (i.e., throttling) on messages from new IP addresses to limit any potential negative impact until the IP address builds up a sending history. This is why it is necessary to warm up a new IP address.

AUTHENTICATION: This allows mailbox providers to associate an identity with a sender and gives them the ability to measure and track a sender's reputation. Mailbox providers check for SPF, DKIM, and DMARC records on incoming mail to separate legitimate messages from emails spoofing brands. Messages that are authenticated by all three protocols may see less filtering and better inbox placement as they will be the most trusted.

SPAM TRAP: These email addresses are old, unused, and/or possibly even created to be traps (hence the name) by mailbox providers and anti-spam organizations to catch spammers and people who send to purchased lists. These are email addresses that never signed up to receive communications (AKA honeypots) or emails that haven't been used recently (AKA recycled spam traps), but both pose a threat to your sending reputation.

MAILBOX PROVIDERS: These include AOL Mail, Outlook.com Mail, Yahoo Mail, and Gmail; these are the most popular web-based email providers.

EMAIL SERVICE PROVIDER (ESP): This is a service that enables marketers to send email marketing campaigns to a list of subscribers. Klaviyo is an example of an ESP.

DELIVERY: A delivery is recorded when a request to send an email results in the receipt of that email by the end recipient. Delivered means the message was accepted by the receiving server. However, this does not necessarily mean that the message reached the recipient's inbox. Did you know the industry average delivery rate is 82%?

DELIVERABILITY: This is a term that refers to inbox placement once an email is successfully delivered. This term is often used interchangeably with delivery, which refers to whether a recipient's inbox accepts the message you've sent. Only after an email is successfully delivered does deliverability come into play.

DOMAIN NAME SYSTEM (DNS): This system is essentially the "phone book of the Web." When you update your DNS records, you can consider this the equivalent of updating your address in the web's phonebook so that it's possible to verify who you are when you send an email.

DOMAIN KEYS IDENTIFIED MAIL (DKIM): This is a protocol that allows an organization to take responsibility for transmitting a message by signing it in a way that mailbox providers can verify. It leaves a digital signature on every outgoing message, which lets receiving servers verify the message actually came from your organization.

SENDER POLICY FRAMEWORK (SPF): This is a protocol that domain owners use to specify the email servers and domains that are authorized to send email on behalf of your organization.

DOMAIN-BASED MESSAGE AUTHENTICATION, RE-PORTING, and CONFORMANCE (DMARC): This tells receiving servers what to do with outgoing messages from your organization that don't pass SPF or DKIM.

SIMPLE MAIL TRANSFER PROTOCOL (SMTP): This is an application used by mail servers to send, receive, and/or relay outgoing mail between email senders and receivers.

Email Deliverability is the sum of multiple technical and non-technical variables. There is no clear-cut solution to deliverability problems due to the wide range of contributing factors; therefore, you must understand the variables in order to work out a solution to your problem.

Deliverability is important to you because you want your emails to arrive in the inbox when and how you'd expect. With poor practices, your emails will likely be routed to the spam folder or completely blocked by mailbox providers.

And, likely most important to you, poor deliverability = low (or no) ROI. If people aren't receiving your emails, they aren't buying.

As mailbox providers get savvier, hitting the inbox is not as easy as it once was; advanced machine learning is only making filtering systems more impressive and difficult to penetrate without best practices.

In this chapter, we'll be going through the key aspects of deliverability.

- Sender Reputation
- User Experience
- Infrastructure + Authentication
- Compliance + Privacy
- Tools

Sender Reputation

Your sender reputation is a major factor in your email deliverability. The better your reputation, the more likely you are to have a higher delivery rate. Your reputation is determined by quite a wide variety of factors:

- Recipient engagement *[priority]*
- Domain & IP reputation
- List health
- Email content
- Blacklists

Recipient Engagement

Your subscribers' responses to your emails matter—a lot. It's critical that you follow best practices, such as adjusting your segmentation to meet the criteria that your Email Service Provider (ESP) has laid out for you. The actions your subscribers take let mailbox providers know whether or not your emails are welcome.

Sample from Klaviyo:

	UNIQUE OPEN RATES	UNIQUE CLICK RATES	BOUNCE RATES	UNSUBSCRIBE RATES	SPAM RATES
Great	35% or more	2.5% or more	Less than 0.4%	Less than 0.2%	Less than 0.05%
Proficient	25-30%	1.5-2.5%	0.4-0.8%	0.2-0.3%	0.05-0.08%
Room for Improvement	20-25%	1-1.5%	0.8-1.5%	0.3-0.7%	0.08-0.15%
Critical	Less than 20%	Less than 1%	1.5% or more	0.7% or more	0.15% or more

If your open rates are below 20%, you can assume some of your emails are going to spam. If your open rates are below 15%, you definitely have emails going to spam.

Opens, clicks, bounces, unsubscribes, and spam rate are not the only actions that inbox providers are tracking. They may also be tracking whether messages are forwarded, deleted, or moved to another folder. Actually, I've heard recently that Gmail tracks whether or not someone scrolls down through the entire email and that more than one mailbox provider is now tracking the amount of time subscribers have each email open as well. There are so many factors in the ways that mailbox providers track actions that we will never gain access to— and they all have their own ways of tracking and measuring things!

The weight of each action will never be 100% clear, but keeping a close eye on your delivery and deliverability metrics can help you continue to adjust and keep up with the ever-evolving mailbox providers.

More simply put, the actions that each recipient takes are a bit like casting votes.

I like the analogy that James Clear uses in his book *Atomic Habits* when comparing casting votes to creating a change in an identity.

"Every action you take is a vote for the type of person you wish to become. No single instance will transform your beliefs, but as the votes build up, so does the evidence of your new identity."[1]

Email Deliverability kind of works in this way as well. Each action a recipient takes (their "votes") is pushing your deliverability in a more positive or less positive direction. It can be a positive vote (opening, clicking, forwarding, replying), or it can be a negative vote (marking as spam, unsubscribing, not opening, not clicking).

We know that negative "votes" carry much more weight than positive votes, but because it is unclear how the mailbox providers measure these "votes," it becomes even more important to ensure that you are mitigating the negative actions as much as possible.

At the time of writing this, we are nearly a year into the iOS15 rollout (from Sept. 2021) that caused such a ruckus amongst marketers (and not just the email marketers).

What you need to know about iOS15 in regard to email marketing:

Apple's Mail Privacy Protection (MPP) update gave users the option to use three major components that affect email marketing:

- The ability to turn off open tracking
- The ability to block your IP address
- The ability to hide your email address (which was actually previously available)

And what we are ACTUALLY seeing as the impact so far:

- Open rates were already a vanity metric and now even more so—they are inflated (inflation rates vary from list to list—some have seen very subtle effects while others have seen massive changes).
- Click-through rates are appearing to be lower than they actually are due to the inflated open rates.

In reality, this just means that your email marketer needs to be even more knowledgeable about deliverability than in the past. Clicks and conversions are still king when reading data from individual emails.

We're still playing the same game; the rules have just changed slightly. ;)

And DID YOU KNOW that machine opens happen *only* under the following conditions:

- On an iPhone
- Using Apple Mail App (this is the standard built-in email application on an iPhone)
- When the phone is plugged in
- When the phone is on Wi-Fi
- When the subscriber has explicitly opted in to the mail privacy feature – apparently stats are currently showing over 90% of people who have upgraded to ios15 have opted in to this.

> All of these conditions must be met in order for a machine open to occur—this gives some insight into the reason why open rates often shoot up in the evenings or overnight—people are at home with Wi-Fi and are plugging their phones in as they get ready for bed.

List Health

Maintaining list health is not an option—it's a must. As I mentioned previously, your deliverability is going to directly affect the ROI of your marketing program. Your list health plays a huge role in this.

Tips to make sure you have a healthy subscriber list:

- NEVER purchase a list or scrape one together.
  - Not only is this against most, if not all, reputable ESPs' terms of service, but it's a quick way to fill your list with the WRONG people who are not going to convert but who are likely to take actions that harm your deliverability (unsubscribing, marketing as spam, unengaged, etc.).
- Send emails ONLY to those who have opted in (either directly or indirectly via a purchase).
- Honor requests to unsubscribe. ESPs will generally suppress unsubscribed profiles automatically if an "unsubscribe" button is clicked, but we often see complaints from customers who called in or replied to an email asking directly—in these cases, you

must manually ensure those folks have been unsubscribed.

- Run unengaged subscribers through a list-cleaning software on an annual basis (or more frequently if necessary for your volume of traffic/subscribers).
- Set up semi-automated list cleaning solutions like the "sunset flow," which you'll read about in Section 3 on flow automations.
- Segment your subscribers! Ensure you're sending to an engaged segment that is allowing you to achieve the open rates that will keep your deliverability high.
- Segment subscribers out based on sales cycle. For example, if your customers come back every 75 days to make a purchase, you can exclude them from a number of your regular sends, if not all of them, for a certain period of time. Unless you're sending relevant and educational content that they'd like to see, there is no sense in burning them out right after they make a purchase.

Expert tip regarding ASKING people to unsubscribe (really only helpful in extreme situations – good email practices would not put you in a situation where you need to use this):

The "FAUX NO"

There are some instances where you may want to ask your unengaged subscribers or non-buyers to unsub-

---

scribe. Using this trick is a great alternative to getting a REAL unsubscribe or a spam complaint.

Generally, list cleaning emails are set up as automations like the "sunset flow," so you can slowly feed unengaged subscribers through rather than blasting a group of them with a campaign and getting bad marks towards your deliverability score.

Years ago, my team created what we call the "Faux Unsubscribe Button."

You can place it at the top of the email where it will be the first thing your subscribers see.

Instead of linking the button to an unsubscribe merge tag that creates a true "unsubscribe," we link it to a landing page and have a segment set up on the backend to capture their email address. (You still need to include the real unsubscribe link at the bottom of your email.)

Per current CAN-SPAM regulations, you have 10 days to unsubscribe someone from your list if they have requested you to do so.

If you use this tactic, you need to stay on top of suppressing these people on, in my opinion, a daily basis. While legally you have 10 days to unsubscribe those that click, you don't want these folks to receive another email and report you or mark your emails as spam.

I put so much emphasis on keeping your list clean because sending emails to recipients who no longer engage with your messages damages your sender reputation for several reasons:

- Addresses that don't open or click on your messages are more likely to mark your messages as spam.
- Unengaged addresses can become spam traps.
- Unengaged recipients can lower your open rates, which make your emails look unwelcomed.

One of the most common issues I see when reviewing deliverability issues is in regard to segmentation/list health … or lack thereof, rather. I've seen too many companies sending their emails to people who haven't engaged in many months or even years.

Not only is this bad practice, but it also costs money to store and send to those unengaged email addresses. Save money and stop sending to them or suppress them all together!

Important note for B2B retailers:

There are a couple of factors unique to B2B that you should keep in mind. Businesses (and especially their individual employees) come and go, and that often means the emails associated with that business or those folks become non-existent. You'll want to keep up with your list cleaning tactics (using a cleaning software, sunsetting, etc.) to make sure you're not sending messages to business email addresses that either no longer exist or are no longer in use.

Blacklists aka Blocklists

Not all blacklists are created equal. Some carry significant weight (Spamhaus), while others may not cause any noticeable effect at all. Many mailbox providers utilize blacklists to help determine which senders need to be filtered or completely blocked. Mailbox providers will also block domains on their own, so blacklists are not the only issue.

Most blacklists will list your IP address or sending domain if they notice a high number of spam trap receipts or spam complaints. Another good reason to keep your list clean!

On the bright side, reputable ESPs like Klaviyo actually monitor these blacklists for you. There are also a number of fail-safes in place to alert your marketing team of an issue before things get this dire. Here are a couple of examples of what might lead you to recognize an issue:

1. You notice campaign data is not in alignment with your ESP recommendations, particularly when it comes to open rates, spam complaints, and bounces.
2. You get a warning from your ESP for data that falls within their designated "critical" range, like an email getting more than x% bounce rate, for example — whatever those thresholds are.

There are many little tips within the data that can lead you to discover issues. You just need to be aware of the parameters so you can recognize when there are issues that, ultimately, will allow you to course correct.

If you'd like to check to see whether or not you're on any blacklists, you can use the free lookup tool by MX-ToolBox. Remember, just because you're on a blacklist doesn't necessarily equate to a noticeably negative impact on deliverability. There are hundreds of them, and some are not even utilized by mailbox providers.

If you do find that you are on a blacklist, the list in question will likely have instructions on their site regarding how to request removal of your domain, but it does generally require some sort of verification and will then call for higher monitoring of your domain in the near future once removed. For those that don't have instructions on the site, it's a good idea to contact the owner of the blacklist to explain your situation.

User Experience

Not to negate the importance of any of what I've explained regarding sender reputation, but the truth is that emails that customers love make it to the inbox.

Both aspects are important—you can use the best practices in the world in terms of deliverability, but if you're sending garbage email content (visually unappealing, not relative to the recipient, etc.), the garbage is exactly where those emails are going to end up.

"To a great extent, email deliverability is self-fulfilling. If you send content that your audience wants to receive and

that they find interesting, the algorithms will learn that your email should be delivered to the inbox.

If you send email that wasn't asked for and doesn't deliver value, your recipients will act in a passive or negative way, and the algorithms that control filtering will learn to deliver your email to the junk folder. Of course, there are other influencing factors that contribute to email success, but ultimately, if you send email that people love, it will be successful."

– Dale Langley, Deliverability Consulting Lead, EMEA & APJ @ SendGrid

Infrastructure + Authentication

Infrastructure refers to the IP address(es) and server(s) you're using to send email. Authentication refers to the validation techniques you use to show that you truly own the email coming from you.

Let's start with authentication basics and the topic I get asked about most frequently—SPF, DKIM, and DMARC.

Authentication

To understand why these are so important, we need to go back about 40 years to a time before email was used as a commercial tool.

At its inception, email was primarily used as a tool by professors, researchers, and academics to share ideas and information—there was no reason to be concerned about crime or even that this tool would someday be utilized commercially.

Because email was built as an open tool with no security protocols, security has been bolted on after the fact.

Why did security protocols need to be implemented anyway? Well … did you know that roughly 85% of the email being sent today is spam? It's quite a surprise to many because the average person never sees a majority of it—it doesn't even make it into the "spam" section of our inboxes.

Yes, you read that right. Not a typo. 85%. There is a constant battle between spammers and mailbox providers that marketers just happen to be caught in the middle of.

Mailbox providers are fighting HARD to keep out the bad stuff and to only show the good stuff—this is why we have to work so hard to maintain high deliverability. Mailbox providers aren't making things difficult just for fun. There is a much bigger, more nefarious enemy that they are fighting.

That's where SPF, DKIM, and DMARC come into play. I've included their descriptions in the "Words to Know," but let's break it down a little bit further.

SPF and DKIM are protocols that were built to achieve the same goal, to prove their origin's trustworthiness and verify to mailbox providers that the email is "safe." The two protocols just go about this in different ways.

You can think of SPF as having two sides to it:

1. The "friendly" from address
2. The "backend" from address

The "friendly" from address, for example, is karly@email-isnotdead.co. The backend address is what verifies that it and the "friendly" address are who they say they are. Essentially this backend address redirects the receiving server to check the TXT record in the sender's DNS server. A proper SPF setup will list all approved servers mail is allowed to come from. If that particular IP is not on the list, the SPF check will fail.

DKIM, on the other hand, uses asymmetric encryption to generate a public and private key pair. The private key is used to create a unique signature for each email. When the email gets unencrypted by a mailbox provider on the receiving end, the mailbox provider's server checks the DNS records of the sender to verify the public key TXT record. Using that public key, the server can verify whether the email was actually sent by the domain it claims or if it was altered in transit. If this check fails, the email could be marked as spam or blocked altogether.

Simply put, the DKIM protocol is another way of verifying origin, building trust, and proving to an automated system that it should be allowed entry.

DMARC works with SPF and DKIM to further protect your domain. It essentially works as the gatekeeper for the receiving server.

When an email arrives to a receiving server that doesn't pass the SPF or DKIM check, the DMARC settings tell the receiver what to do with it—reject, monitor, or quarantine.

DMARC isn't mandatory, but it can help you authenticate the emails you are sending and fight spammers by ensuring fraudulent email is not getting delivered.

Infrastructure

Domain & IP Reputation

Your IP address and sending domain are equally important. Before I get into specifics, I want to explain what I mean when I talk about domains (dedicated vs. shared) and IP addresses (shared vs. dedicated).

Shared IPs vs. Dedicated IPs

If you are sending via an ESP, you are likely sending from a shared IP. This means that your sending practices and subscriber engagement are not the only factors taken into account by the mailbox providers. All other senders in your IP pool are affecting its reputation with their sending habits as well.

For most retailers, this is a positive thing. No, you do not have complete control over the reputation of your IP… but it's generally a good thing that you don't. If you don't have a high sending volume that is consistent, you need to rely on others around you to maintain your IPs reputation. That being said, you'll want to be on your very best behavior in terms of sending habits so that you're grouped in with others of similar stature.

It is much rarer for a retailer to be in a position to move to a dedicated IP as they not only need a high volume, but they also need to ensure they have a staff of high-level email marketing experts to ensure continued excellence.

Dedicated vs. Shared Domains

Setting up a dedicated sending domain with your ESP ensures that emails appear to come from your brand rather than the ESP. Companies tend to do this to streamline their branding, but it can also improve sending reputation as well.

In simple terms, this means that the from address will match your domain.

Shared Domain Example:

Dedicated Domain Example:

What does setting up a dedicated sending domain do for you?

Let's backtrack a little bit to talk about DKIM again. What I have not yet explained is that DKIM carries a stamp. This stamp is either first- or third-party.

First-party/dedicated domain: I am sending this email.

Third-party/shared domain: Karly is sending this email.

When you are using a shared domain, you are using a third-party stamp. Once you switch to a dedicated domain, you are using a first-party stamp.

We want to show a first-party stamp because mailbox providers, especially Gmail, are finding it more reputable.

In addition, when you set up your dedicated domain, DMARC should be automatically applied as well. DMARC is applied with the "friendly from" that matches the domain being utilized for the DKIM setup. In simple terms, your from address, i.e., karly@emailisnotdead.co, now actually matches the domain that is sending the email, and, therefore, DMARC is now helping your reputation with inbox providers as well.

And, contrary to popular belief, if you are not currently having any deliverability issues and you switch to a dedicated domain, you do NOT have to warm it up.

One of the best examples I can share of how important *both* IP and domain reputation are is that of a past client that was sending cold email from their primary domain via another platform. Facepalm.

Why the facepalm? Cold emails notoriously have low open rates and click rates with high spam and unsubscribe rates. Exactly the opposite that you'd want to show in order to build your reputation.

So, regardless of this client's best sending practices within their eCommerce store's ESP, they could not figure out why their emails were going to spam. In this case, regardless of sending excellent content to only the most engaged subscribers, they were unknowingly trashing their domain on another platform in the form of cold email. Mystery solved.

If messages sent from your domain are generating negative responses, it won't matter (or will matter much less) which IP address they are coming from.

Expert Tip (for larger brands):

To further increase your brand recognition, boost open rates, and build trust with your subscribers, consider implementing BIMI (Brand Indicators for Message Identification).

To set up BIMI is to display your brand's logo in recipients' inboxes next to your from address.

There are a few qualifications you'll want to be aware of before making this update:

- The process of implementation can take quite some time.
- Your logo must be trademarked in any country where your BIMI logo will display.
- You must have your DMARC policy set to quarantine or reject.

- You must have a "Verified Mark Certificate" that will cost around $1,500 per year. (Google requires this.)
- You must have a high sending volume. (Yahoo's requirement.)

Google has only recently started using BIMI in general release, but some other mailbox providers like Yahoo have offered it for quite some time.

Compliance + Privacy

For legal reasons, I will not go too far into the specifics of worldwide legislation in regard to email marketing. Even aside from legal reasons, the realm of compliance and privacy is constantly evolving. You will want to make sure that you or your email marketing manager is familiar with all laws and regulations that may be applicable to you.

Fun fact—did you know that many laws apply based on where your subscriber is based rather than where you are based? As if it wasn't already difficult enough!

Some of the most common articles of legislation you may need to be familiar with:

North America

- CAN SPAM
- HIPAA (Health Insurance Portability and Accountability Act)
- EU-US Privacy Shield
- COPPA (California Online Privacy Protection Act)
- CASL (Canadian Anti-Spam Law)

Europe

- GDPR (General Data Protection Regulation)
- EU Opt-in Directive
- EU-US Privacy Shield
- DPA (Data Protection Act)
- + many more for individual countries

Australia

- Spam Act

Tools

DNS Settings Check:

- MX Toolbox*

*DNS.google is a more advanced option.

**MX Toolbox can also be used to check to see if your domain is on any blacklists.

Deliverability Monitoring:

- Google Postmaster*
- Outlook Postmaster*
- ESP Data

If your email marketing team thoroughly understands deliverability and how to read data, deliverability tools like Google and Outlook Postmaster are less helpful.

Testing (Render):

- Litmus
- Email on Acid
- + many more!

List Verification:

- Kickbox
- EmailListVerify
- + many more!

Your Deliverability Audit

Note: Use the white space in this book to make notes and dog-ear the page if you need to come back to it.

Sender Reputation

- ☐ I know which tools are sending emails on behalf of my domain and am comfortable with practices on each of them. (No cold email from your domain!)
- ☐ I am not sending to a list that contains purchased or scraped emails.
- ☐ I have recently cleaned my list.
- ☐ I am sending my campaigns to an engaged segment that shows proficient metrics in opens, clicks, unsubscribes, spam complaints, and bounce rates.
- ☐ I checked mxtoolbox.com [for free] to see if my domain comes up on any major blacklists.

Infrastructure + Authentication

- ☐ I am confident my DNS records are properly set up
  - ☐ SPF
  - ☐ DKIM
  - ☐ DMARC
- ☐ I am set up on a _____ IP (Dedicated or Shared).
- ☐ I have my dedicated domain set up.
- ☐ I have set up BIMI, if appropriate for my brand.

Compliance + Privacy

- ☐ I am aware of every entry point where my customers are opting in.
- ☐ I only send email to those that have opted in.
- ☐ I am aware of and compliant with the laws and regulations that govern my email marketing activity.
- ☐ I manually unsubscribe those who give written or verbal notice.

This chapter does not cover anything related to SMS—see Chapter 6 for information regarding SMS/MMS.

CHAPTER 2

List Building

Words to Know

ZERO PARTY DATA: Data that a customer intentionally and proactively shares with a brand. For example, answers given in an on-site quiz.

FIRST-PARTY DATA: Data stored by the website a consumer visits to customize and improve the customer's experience. These cookies allow the site to remember user preferences and better understand visitor behavior. Want to try this out? Go to Amazon's website and notice that you're probably already logged in. If so, this is the perfect example of first-party data.

THIRD-PARTY DATA: Data collected by a business or other entity that doesn't have any direct link to the visitor or customer. These cookies are placed on websites, usually via a tag or script, and are generally utilized for things like retargeting ads.

CUSTOMER DATA PLATFORM (CDP): Software that combines data from multiple sources to create a single centralized customer database that contains all interactions made with your brand via those tools. (Hint: Klaviyo)

MULTI-STEP POPUP: A popup that has more than one step for collecting information (i.e., The first step might collect a name and email address while the second step collects a phone number).

TEASER: A small widget that a site visitor can click to open a signup form.

FLYOUT: A flyout form will "fly out" from the side of your website after a set delay period.

LEAD MAGNET: A free item or service that is given away for the purpose of gathering contact information.

When talking about list building, it's important to reference Apple and Google's consumer-first privacy updates to set the stage.

For context, these two are incredibly important because Apple has 60+% of market share on mobile phones in the U.S., and Google Chrome has the largest market share for browsers.

Whether it's Apple's crackdown on privacy already in motion or Google's commitment to blocking third-party cookies in 2023 …

We know that third-party tracking is on its way out and that it's crucial for brands to do these four things:

1. Capture site visitors' contact information on the first visit.
2. Rely more on first-party data, less on third-party data.
3. Gather as much zero-party data as possible.
4. Use an ESP that is also a strong CDP platform (Hint: Klaviyo).

Why, you ask?

1. Capture site visitors' contact information on the first visit.

With third-party retargeting options dwindling, it's not as easy to direct users back to your site. While alternative options are surfacing, they may not be quite as ROI positive as Facebook and Instagram ads once were. And why NOT do your best to capture more visitors their first time around?

2. Rely on your own first-party data.

   This is where Klaviyo and their integration partners like Gatsby come into play (point 4). You may not have previously appreciated all the ways in which you actually are gathering data from your customers—POS systems, surveys, reviews, NPS ratings, returns, shipping, and so many other sources!

3. Gather as much zero-party data as possible.

   Zero-party data is certainly a newer term on the block, but there is a reason it's picking up traction. When utilizing software like Octane AI for on-site/in popup quizzes, you can save your customers' responses directly to their email profiles to later (or immediately) use for a more tailored customer journey.

4. Use an ESP that is also a strong CDP platform like Klaviyo.

   Utilizing an email marketing platform (the core of your lifecycle and retention marketing) that integrates with every other software in your tech stack and unifies the data all in one place? Sign me up!

With this in mind, I'll review some of the most common ways to build your list.

List Building

The first thing that always comes up in conversation? Conversion rates. Now, I do have some experience with A/B testing, but I felt the need to get the opinion of a real split-testing mega brain on this one ... that's where Dylan Ander comes in.

For reference, Dylan is the CEO and founder of SplitTesting.com.

Dylan and I are both data junkies. Neither of us likes to make *any* claims unless we are certain that the information we are sharing has some sort of reference, experience, or data to back it up.

Considering this, you can see why I spent 600+ hours on this book AFTER spending 4+ years leading the email marketing strategy on literally hundreds of stores.

... And why I wanted to get Dylan involved in recommendations for this chapter.

So, taking my experience and Dylan's data, we can agree on the following suggestions ...

Quizzes

Why are quizzes, by far, my favorite option for list building?

Most importantly, they allow you to collect zero-party data that you can use to customize the welcome experience and increase initial conversions. Quiz popups also tend to get more interaction than traditional popups.

Here's an example of some basic data gathered by a traditional popup upon signup on a skincare site:

First Name	Karly
Email Address	karly@tequilasunrise.co
Phone Number	(604) 812 - 5828
Location	Canada

Side note—Some ESPs, like Klaviyo, can now predict gender. I've tested it out, and it actually works pretty well; they use census data and the first name to make a determination.

Here's an example of the data gathered by a powerful survey-based popup utilizing Octane AI's software:

First Name	Karly
Email Address	karly@tequilasunrise.co
Phone Number	(604) 812 - 5828
Location	Canada
Skin Type	Combination
Skin Concern	Aging
Age	28
Gender	Female
Allergies	Some fragrances

Customization and better targeting extend so much further than the welcome flow. For example, if this brand was putting together their strategy for a sale campaign, they'd now be able to better tailor it to their audience in a multitude of ways—skin type, skin concern, recipient age, recipient gender, allergens, etc. Like I said, … powerful.

I don't want to skip over the fact that quizzes are also a great way to help your customers find the best solutions for themselves—it's not just a great way to gather their email addresses.

Here is a great example to look at. This brand has a number of quizzes (and guides) on their site. They have been slightly skewed to hide the brand's identity but solidify my point just the same.

Industry: Cosmetics

A few of their on-site guides and quizzes:

- Eyeshadow Quiz
- Foundation Quiz
- Brow Quiz
- Guide to Lipstick
- Clean Foundation Guide
- Best Eyeshadow Under $25

There are actually close to 25 quizzes and guides on this site—you can bet they didn't put in so much effort to build them out if it wasn't working.

Quizzes can be utilized on your home page, throughout the site, or within popups —what questions would you ask your customers?

Popups and Flyouts

Popups and flyouts come in many shapes and sizes. And you now know that quizzes are a great option content-wise, but what else can you do?

Note that the examples shared below can also be implemented as a flyout. Flyouts are less intrusive but also tend to convert at a lower rate.

Traditional / Exit Intent

Traditional and/or exit-intent popups are often used to capture email addresses when a new, non-subscribed visitor comes to the site.

You'll most commonly see these popups with some sort of offer or discount, as this angle converts higher than simply asking someone to join your mailing list. You need to trade something valuable (not necessarily a discount) in exchange for their email address and/or phone number.

Here's an example from one of Dylan's supplement stores that performs really well:

Step 1:

Step 2:

Step 3:

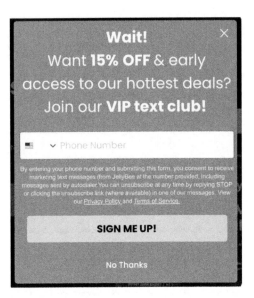

Step 4:

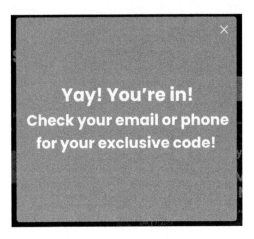

At first glance, you might be thinking that the extra click in the beginning ("yes" or "no") would lead to lower conversion rates, but the truth is that it's actually creating a micro-commitment that leads to higher conversion rates.

This sample from Dylan's site is an EXIT INTENT popup. He actually doesn't use "traditional" popups for a couple of reasons:

- Intrusive (traditional) popups bring your ranking down on Google
- He doesn't want to give discounts to people who are already going to buy

Here's an example from Justuno of an exit-intent popup you can put up in the weeks leading up to Black Friday[2]:

Some email marketers suggest that you can increase conversions further by adding a countdown timer. I personally don't use this tactic right now, but hey, they say it works!

Expert Tip from Dylan:

The best brands in the world always change their popup for the upcoming relevant cycle. Specific single-day sales tend to be harder, but things like "back to school XYZ" or "spring discount ABC" tend to increase conversions.

My hypothesis is that this subconsciously communicates to the consumer that "the brand is 'living'"

Gamified

"Spin Wheel popups are the thing that every marketer hates that works."

– Dylan Ander, Frustrated Marketer

I understand that gamified popups just don't work for some brands. They can also sometimes come off as cheesy, but for some brands, it fits really well. Actually, the highest opt-in rate I've ever seen has come from a "Spin the Wheel" popup.

And the second highest opt-in rate I've ever seen was from Dylan's mobile exit-intent popup shown previously:

List	Submitted Form	Form Submit Rate
10% Off Welcome Popup (JustUno), SMS Subscribers	36	6.9%
10% Off Welcome Popup (JustUno), SMS Subscribers	341	20.1%

A note from Dylan on this opt-in rate, "One of the reasons exit intent opt-in rates will always be higher is because FEWER people are seeing the popup. This doesn't show overall volume; it just shows a percentage opt-in rate, which can be a very misleading metric."

If a wheel works with your brand, it's worth a test.

Targeting and Behavior[3]

As you think through the possibilities of what would work well on your site, consider the variables you can play with to create specific experiences.

- Timing: Popup or flyout show after X # of seconds, after scrolling X % of the page, or on exit intent
- Frequency: Popup disappears forever if someone fills it out, show it to them again every time they

visit if they haven't filled it out, and show again X days after closing it out

- Device: Desktop only, mobile only, or both
- Subscriber Status: Are they already on your list?
- By URL: Which page of the site are they on (or not on)?
- Location: Where are they based?
- Specific Existing Subscribers: Do you only want to show to a specific list or segment of people?

And these are just the basics! There are many popup tools out there, like Justuno, that get more sophisticated and can further target by things like[4]:

- Referral URL
- First URL visitor came to this session
- Number of pages visited this visit
- Number of pages viewed all time
- Days since visitor last engaged this promotion
- Days since visitor last saw specific promotion
- Visitors language settings
- Region/state visitor is currently located in
- Zip code user is currently located in (U.S.)
- Visitors local date
- Visitors local day of the week
- Visitors local time
- Idle user
- Item added to cart this visit
- Item added to cart last 7 days

- Cart total this visit
- Item purchased before
- Purchased (Total Qty/Days/Total Amount)

Expert Tip from Dylan:

Something that works well for ecom brands is making popups custom PER PRODUCT PAGE (PDP).

If you're viewing running shoes, having a popup reflecting running shoes gets a higher opt-in.

Make an offer like "want 10% off any running shoes in our store?"

On-Click Guides:

Declutter your product pages (and others) by utilizing on-click guides like this one from a big clothing brand:

Site:

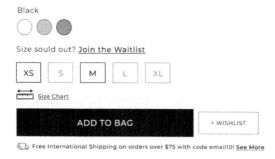

The popup after clicking "Size Chart":

SIZE	US/CAN	BUST	WAIST	HIPS
XXS	00	30.5"-31"	23"-23.5"	33"-33.5"
XS	0	31"-32"	24"-25"	34"-35"
S	2-4	33"-34"	26"-27"	36"-37"
M	6-8	35"-36"	28"-29"	38"-39"
L	10-12	37"-39"	30"-32"	40"-42"
XL	14-16	40"-42"	33"-35"	43"-45"
1X	16-18	43"-45"	36"-38"	46"-48"
2X	20-22	46"-47"	39"-40"	49"-50"
3X	22-24	48"-50"	41"-43"	51"-53"

Gather More Data From Existing Customers:

Here are a couple of the most popular examples of this.

- Build a segment of your email-only customers to collect SMS consent as well
- Collect existing customers' DOBs in order to utilize a "Birthday Flow"

Emerging trend: Collect Instagram and TikTok handles after checkout to build community and scale influencer or ambassador programs (often with Gatsby integration). Here's a great example from Kulani Kinis:

Lead Magnet

Consider the information your potential customers will find relevant—here are some examples:

Product(s)	Lead Magnet Topic
Quit-Smoking Kit	Free "Quit Smoking" 5-Minute Hypnotherapy Session (mp4 download)
Gift Baskets	[Free Download] Guide: What Your Gift Says About You—How to Choose the Perfect Basket
Protein Powder	Free e-Book: Best High-Protein Dessert Recipes
Face Creams	Get the Guide: 5 Anti-aging Myths Everyone Should Know About

Important notes to consider when setting up your popups/flyouts:

1. Use different variations for desktop and mobile. Mobile use is only getting more popular, and, too often, I see that brands are not optimizing for mobile.
2. Utilizing multi-step popups can help you gather more information without the risk of decreasing your signup rate.
3. Utilize teasers that provide greater visibility to your popup.
4. Continuously split test your popup(s).
5. Remember that you can exclude segments of your list or target specific subscribers and/or customers. For example, if you have a welcome offer you only want to show to new visitors, you can exclude existing customers from seeing the form.

What is a "good" opt-in rate for your popup?
First, it's important to consider a few things:

- Not all tools calculate this number in the same way.
- Not all forms have the same purpose.
- Not all traffic is created equal.
- Not all popups are created equal.

Every platform that has popup-hosting capabilities has a different answer to this question too.

Klaviyo:

"While what 'good' means for each form will differ depending on the purpose of the form, the median form submit rate for popups and flyouts is only 2.3%. Most successful forms have between a 1 and 3% form submit rate, but extremely high performing forms can have up to a 6.5% form submit rate."[5]

Note that this is the AVERAGE on the platform. Remember that most brands do not have a professional agency or marketer advising their strategies, so you should definitely always aim higher than the average!

Sumo:

"The average email opt-in rate is 1.95%. Anything above that, and you're doing better than half the world. Nice work :) This statistic is based on over 3.2 BILLION people who have seen our email capture popups. So it's pretty accurate. And statistics say you or the person next to you have seen our tools in action."[6]

"The top 10% highest-performing popups averaged a 9.28% conversion rate. And, by conversion rate, we mean someone who saw a popup and took action. Only 3 out of 100 people ever have popups with conversion rates over 11%."[7]

OptiMonk:

"According to our results, the average popup conversion rate is 11.09%. But you shouldn't be disappointed if one of your campaigns was below this conversion rate. When and how a popup is used makes a big difference to conversion rates. For example, a newsletter popup typically converts way less than a cart abandonment popup. That's because customers are in very different stages of your conversion funnel."[8]

Campaign Monitor:

"While the average conversion rate for popups is 3.09%, the top popups have almost 10% conversion rates. Of those top-performing popups, 92% of them have popups that display after 4 seconds. The lowest-performing displayed their ads between 0 and 4 seconds."[9]

Long story short, there isn't a "standard" answer for this question. This is because the range varies so widely. There are many factors involved—the quality of traffic, popup design, popup copy/CTA, popup offer, popup behavior, etc. Keep testing and keep trying to increase that percentage. Set goals based on your own benchmarks.

And remember that every company is *probably* marketing themselves in some way when they are putting together blog posts and articles. I personally would be SHOCKED if the platform you were using for your popup made any difference in the opt-in rate, assuming all factors were the same.

On a personal note—I generally work off of Klaviyo's recommendation in terms of opt-in percentages because their data is based on Klaviyo customers, who are primarily eCommerce brands. But again, professionals should be shooting above that average.

Here's some more specific data from Klaviyo's research on popups based on data from more than 80,000 businesses utilizing their platform:

- Popup forms convert at a higher rate (3.2%) than flyout forms (2.2%).
- The top 10% of signup forms have submission rates of over 6%.
- 85% of forms have two fields or less.
- But, forms with up to five fields only see a small dip in conversion (<0.1%).
- Forms have higher submission rates on mobile (3.2%) than on desktop (2.3%).
- Forms asking for phone numbers and emails see similar submission rates (2.9%) compared to email-only forms (2.7%).

Here's their breakdown of conversion rate by form type:

FORM TYPE	AVERAGE CONVERSION RATE	90TH PERCENTILE CONVERSION RATE
Embedded	0.3%	24.7%*
Flyout	2.2%	6.1%
Popup	3.2%	7.8%

Note: This high conversion rate is likely due to the fact that the most successful embedded forms tend to be on high-converting landing pages (e.g., high-stakes contests) rather than general-purpose or product pages.

Klaviyo's research also shows that mobile users are more likely to submit a form than desktop users:

DEVICE TYPE	AVERAGE CONVERSION RATE
Mobile	3.4%
Desktop	2.4%

BUT the information I found most interesting is in regard to research around the number of fields in popups versus conversion rates. I've always heard, and I'm sure you have as well, that adding additional fields in popups causes the submission rate to drop.

Here's what Klaviyo found:

Most forms utilized through their platform only have one field.

NUMBER OF FIELDS	% OF FORMS
1	55%
2	30%
3	10%
4	4%
5	1%

What's really interesting about it? How much the conversion rate DOESN'T drop when you add additional fields:

NUMBER OF FIELDS	AVERAGE CONVERSION RATE
1	2.73%
2	2.67%
3	2.69%
4	2.61%
5	2.60%

Yes, it does drop, but not as significantly as you'd think.

This was genuinely such a cool study for me to find because I've always been under the impression that additional fields would impact conversion rates much more than they actually do.

So, what else makes for a high-performing popup?

For this question, I want to reference Drip's study on "the right timing" for your popup because this is a question I have been asked literally hundreds of times.

Here's the breakdown from Drip:

"We wanted to find the optimal time to show a popup. So, to do that, we looked at 10+ million popup views. Then, we filtered out any popups with 2,000 views or less to ensure our overall conversion rate was valid. We had a lot of results with timers ranging from one second to 200 seconds. So, we filtered out the top 10 highest-performing timers by seconds to give us the following (not in order): 30, 4, 3, 6, 5, 8, 7, 15, 10, 20. We found that popups that are shown after eight seconds (3.62) convert better than popups shown before or after."[10]

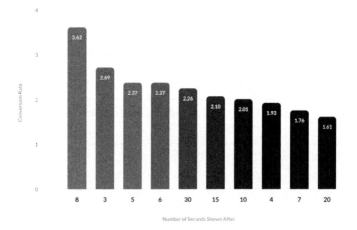

How Many Seconds Should You Wait Until You Show a Popup?

Here are their results of a similar test based on scroll-trigger instead of timing[11]:

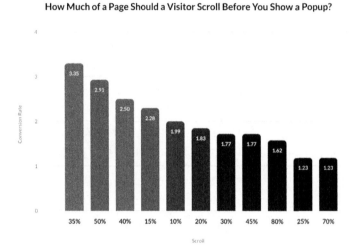

How Much of a Page Should a Visitor Scroll Before You Show a Popup?

Note: You can use a teaser to increase the visibility of your popup. One study showed a visibility increase of 65%![12]

If you do decide to use a teaser, make sure that it doesn't interfere with any other elements on your site—desktop and mobile!

Side note—it was quite entertaining talking to Dylan about timing for popups because he hates them so much. His exact words were, "gun to my head ... if I had to recommend popup timing, I would say to look at your average session time on Google Analytics and place your popup at 85–90% of that."

Embed Forms

The most common embed form you see on eCommerce sites is in the footer (on every page).

The sign-up rates via this option are generally quite low, but consumers have been trained to search in this section when they want to sign up for a newsletter. Don't miss out on these signups because you didn't include this simple form.

These are great because you can funnel these folks into content-based flows that you know they'll actually enjoy.

To put this chapter in a nutshell, you want to mix and match a number of these list-building solutions to grow your list more efficiently and effectively. There is no one-size-fits-all solution—test, test, test!

Expert Tip:

Giveaways run via apps and third parties can seem like a great way to generate more subscribers, but the quality of those subscribers is often very low quality. Yes, people ARE opting into them legally in most cases, but they usually aren't very interested.

Disclaimer: I have never actually taken part in running these myself, but I have heard a lot of negative feedback.

Your List Building Audit

Foundation

- ☐ I am using an ESP that doubles as a CDP, like Klaviyo, so I can fully utilize the zero- and first-party data that I have access to.
- ☐ I am utilizing software that allows me to build my list efficiently and effectively (i.e., I have the tools necessary to create quizzes, targeted popups, etc.).
- ☐ I have all subscriber profiles feeding into a single platform (i.e., My in-store POS system is linked to my ESP).

Popups

- ☐ I am capturing new subscribers that come to my site via a popup.
  - ☐ I have a teaser/widget set up for my popup to maximize visibility.
  - ☐ I am only showing this popup to new visitors and/or non-subscribers.
  - ☐ I am collecting SMS.
  - ☐ I am not showing my popup immediately on page load.
  - ☐ I have optimized versions for both desktop and mobile.
  - ☐ My opt-in rate is __%.

☐   I am happy with my current opt-in rate.

Dylan might disagree with this one, but I'll let you make your own call. ;)

☐   I have an exit-intent popup set up.
    ☐   My offer is overwhelmingly valuable.
    ☐   My opt-in rate is __%.
    ☐   I am happy with my current opt-in rate.
☐   I am collecting additional information from my returning visitors and/or customers that will help me better market to them and segment later on.
☐   I have considered all of the ways I can utilize popups and am confident I am using them to the highest level possible.
☐   I am A/B testing my popup(s).

Embed Forms:

☐   I have an embed form on the footer of my site on every page.
    ☐   My opt-in rate is __%.
☐   I have an embed form on my blog and/or content-based pages.
    ☐   My opt-in rate is __%.
    ☐   I have a special content-based flow built for this segment of subscribers.

I am testing:

- ☐ Timing
- ☐ Offer
- ☐ Design
- ☐ Copy
- ☐ _____ (What are YOU testing?)

Ideas for other ways I could be building my list:

"What goes around comes around. Sometimes you get what's coming around. And sometimes you are what's coming around."

– Jim Butcher

The only way for this book to help people is by reaching them first. Can you please help me do that?

A minute of your time can help another business owner, marketer, or entrepreneur take a step towards improving their email marketing program and, ultimately, their business and life.

I genuinely believe that this book can help anyone who is working in this industry if I can just find a way to get it to them. You must feel that way as well if you've made it this far.

On behalf of those folks, I ask that you take a minute to either:

1) Leave a review on Amazon so others can see how valuable it is.

OR

2) If you know someone personally that it would help, send them a quick text or email with the link to buy it. Or, in an even greater gesture of goodwill, buy it for them.

A minute of your time now can mean so much to others (and me) in distributing this information.

And, a tip that I picked up from Alex Hormozi, did you know that if you introduce something valuable to someone, they associate that value with you? As if you needed another reason to help.

Thank you in advance for your time in helping me with this … but, more importantly, thank you for your time in reading this far into the book. It means so much to me that I can make a difference in another person's life.

CHAPTER 3

Content Basics

Words to Know

DARK MODE: A setting that shifts an interface's color palette to display content in high contrast using dark background colors and light foreground. Black text becomes white, and white backgrounds go dark. Ultimately, dark mode is used to minimize blue light and enhance readability to reduce eye strain.

EMAIL RENDERING: How an email appears across a variety of browsers, mailbox providers, and devices. Email rendering is determined by operating system, ESP settings, screen size, and inbox provider.

"People will do anything for those who encourage their dreams, justify their failures, allay their fears, confirm their suspicions, and help them throw rocks at their enemies."

– Blair Warren

There is a shift happening not just in our society but with marketing in general. Marketers follow the people. The people are showing us that they want what is real and raw. More now than ever, brands need to recognize their customers' need for community and the importance of personalized messaging.

UGC, customer stories, photos of REAL people and not models—this is important to have in mind when designing your email program.

While copywriting and design styles and strategy vary, human psychological triggers never change.

"We are here to connect. Life is about people. Advertising is about illuminating how our products and services will improve people's lives. Now, how do we do that? Love. Time. Death. Now these three abstractions connect every single human being on Earth. Everything that we covet, everything that we fear not having, everything that we ultimately end up buying is because at the end of the day we long for love, we wish we had more time, and we fear death."

– Will Smith as Howard in *Collateral Beauty*

Yes, this quote is from a movie, but it still rings true. Regardless of the methods you are employing in your copywriting or design efforts, the emotions that you are trying to tap into ultimately boil down to some very simple, universal human fears and desires.

And, regardless of your product type or how you spin it, there are proven conversion points in email marketing that will help you drive it home (or to the cart, in our case).

I also want to be clear that in terms of the framework for your emails, there is no single "right" way to do things. What I can share with you is a proven framework for content that we've crafted over thousands and thousands of emails that fosters great results.

I'll also share some of my FAVORITE emails from a brand that doesn't actually follow any of the "rules." Funny how that works!

Framework

Here are a few examples of high-performing frameworks that we use on a regular basis:

1. Indoctrination-based emails like those found in a Welcome flow:

1 — Logo + Navbar

2 — Hero image + header, subheader, coupon when applicable + Main CTA

3 — Intro paragraph

4 — Product/service spotlight +coupon when applicable + Main CTA

5 — Value callouts/Differentiators/ Featured on (when applicable)

6 — Testimonials + Social proof + secondary CTA

7 — Objection handling section (Risk reversals, guarantees, FAQ)

8 — Closing paragraph + coupon when applicable + Main CTA

9 — Questions/Comments/contact us Block (optional)

10 — Footer Sign-off (could contain the slogan or brand mission) with Social media links, Address/Preferences link /Unsubscribe link

2. "Sales Cycle Exit" emails like those found in an Abandoned Cart or Browse Abandonment flow:

3. Content-based emails:

Here are some answers to the questions we get asked most frequently about our framework:

1. Navigation (Header) Links

Q: I've heard that nobody clicks on the header links. Do we need to include them?

A: The answer is that it depends. Yes, the header links get far fewer clicks than a main CTA, as they should, but does that make them unnecessary? Additional clicks on an email can be a positive thing if you're struggling with click rate. You may also have a product that leads customers to have a lot of questions, wherein header links could be particularly helpful.

Some people choose to add their primary links at the bottom of an email so they don't distract from the primary message. My advice is to test it out and see what works best and whether it even makes a noticeable difference for your brand.

2. "Featured On"

Q: Why do you include this section in so many emails?

A: The answer to this one is simple—to build authority. It's most powerful when used in emails that are pushing for an initial purchase but can be a great reminder later in a customer's journey as well.

3. Objection Handling

Q: What is the purpose of this section?

A: We want to take the reasons that people may be afraid to buy from you or that would cause them to buy specifically from you and not a competitor.

We reinforce these triggers, whatever they may be, as a conversion trigger/objection handling. An example of some common factors may be "Made in the USA," "Free Returns," "Organic," "Vegan," "Sustainably Packaged," etc.

4. "Contact Us"

Q: What is the reason for adding a contact and/or FAQ section in every email?

A: This section provides a better customer experience and builds trust. If your brand is not a household name, one of the biggest challenges you face is overcoming your potential customer's fear of buying from you. Even if your subscribers are not actually utilizing your contact information on a regular basis, the simple fact that you've made it easy and *an option* is enough to quash fears.

5. Urgency and/or Countdown Timers

Q: Why is there always a deadline when coupon codes or offers are presented?

A: This isn't just a marketing tactic; it's human psychology. Urgent situations force our brains to make decisions immediately, so instead of allowing time to think about it (and probably forget about it), you force your subscribers to make a decision quickly.

6. Address

Q: Do I have to include my address?

A: Yes, to comply with the CAN-SPAM act, you must include the physical mailing address of your business in every email.

The actual content used in your emails should vary, and there are, of course, other tricks you can use. Understanding the most impactful conversion points is a good place to start when you're considering what you'll need to include in your emails.

Common Issues With Content

Mobile View

Always double-check your emails to make sure they are optimized for mobile. A major chunk of your subscribers (varies by brand, but averaging somewhere around 50%+) are checking email on their phones, and you need to make sure you are providing the intended experience across all devices.

Dark Mode

I'm actually chuckling to myself as I address this issue because it always makes me facepalm.

> *"Dark mode is a user-selected setting, and it is not advisable or possible to completely avoid the impacts of dark mode on your email designs. Instead, it's best to optimize your emails for compatibility with dark mode."*[13]

This is an issue that, if I had to guess, every brand has faced—even if they don't know it. Brands and marketers have gotten a lot better at handling it, though, and there are a few quick tips straight from a Klaviyo help article that can help you mitigate the issues:

- Use transparent backgrounds. Images with background colors might be difficult to see in dark mode. Use transparent backgrounds with all of your images to ensure they are displayed properly.

- Optimize your logo and social icons. If your brand uses dark colors for your logo or social icons, add in a thin white border around it to improve readability. In light mode, users will not see the white border, but in dark mode, they will be able to see your logo and social icons.
- When in doubt, use text. To ensure your message comes through in dark mode, opt for using text rather than images of text. This will not only render better in dark mode but also improve your deliverability and accessibility.
- Test your emails. Send a preview to yourself or use a third-party tool like Litmus.

There are a number of other methods you can employ to help with these issues as well—I'll save you the headache and ask you to Google it instead of spending multiple pages of this book explaining meta tags, special HTML snippets, and CSS hacks.

Outlook Rendering

Outlook is by far the most difficult mailbox provider to format emails properly for.

Optimizing an email specifically for Outlook can take a lot of time and extensive testing, as there are no established guidelines. Doing this also requires making significant changes to how images are positioned, and this can skew how emails render across other email clients and devices.

What exactly is happening?

Outlook has many different versions of its platform that use multiple rendering engines—meaning there isn't one solution to fix rendering across all Outlook inboxes. It does not support CSS styles for widths and heights, does not display images by default until a person turns this feature on, does not support GIFs, does not support interactive content, removes padding and/or margins from images, and much, much more!

On the bright side, an overwhelming majority of the time, Outlook users account for an extremely small percentage of overall recipients—sometimes even less than 1%.

If you decide to take the plunge and find a solution for this problem, you'll be wise to find a developer that is proficient in conditional coding, MSO properties, VML, HTML, and CSS. ;)

The good news is that Outlook announced "One Outlook" in January 2022 to replace desktop clients sometime this year. This issue might eventually have a more simple solution. Hallelujah.

And just to note—I am including this section because it's a common topic/issue that comes up for most brands. But, out of everything I've included in this book, this is one of the least important concepts I'd choose to focus on … unless, for some reason, you have a higher than normal percentage of subscribers utilizing Outlook, which certainly could be the case for B2B sellers, for example.

Custom Fonts

Custom fonts are fun (not!) because they aren't accepted across all mailbox providers—Google and Yahoo, for example, do not support them.

You can absolutely use custom fonts in your emails, but be sure to set a fallback. I actually have to share this awful mistake we made back in 2020 when utilizing a custom font without a fallback. This is a screenshot from that email:

> *THERE'S ONLY 24 HOURS*
> *LEFT FOR EARLY ACCESS TO*
> *BLACK FRIDAY SAVINGS!*

We all died a little inside that day, but it's one of the most memorable mistakes of our agency's entire existence for me. I literally laughed out loud upon finding this email again, but hey, this client is still with us today!

To ensure the font in your emails is rendering equally across platforms, you are best to use a font that is supported by all browsers.

Here are a few of the most popular "safe" fonts, but keep in mind that there are quite a few others:

- Arial
- Verdana
- Helvetica

- Georgia
- Tahoma
- Lucida
- Trebuchet
- Times

If you do decide to use a custom font for those subscribers who CAN see it, make sure to utilize a fallback font that works with the email design as well.

My Favorite Brand

Now … for the grand reveal! Which brand has captured my heart and has me opening every. single. one. of their emails?
Drumroll … birddogs.com!
A couple of very ironic notes about this brand:

1. As I mentioned, they don't follow any of the standard or "proven" email marketing tactics.
2. They sell men's clothing. I don't wear men's clothing. I still buy LOTS of their clothing (for my husband).

Here's a recent subject line that piqued my interest (not that the others don't):

"Who's the Hottest in the Office?"

The intro once you open it:

"BIRDDOGS MOST ELIGIBLE BACHELOR
As ranked by Karl's mom."

Want to know who the hottest in the office was? I sure did. Here's a screenshot straight from the email:

1st Hottest - Jack

Jack is a Dartmouth 10 which means he's a real world 6.

However, being a Dartmouth 10 while at Dartmouth surprisingly gets you the less action than a real world 6.

Honestly, the birddogs emails kill me every time. Apparently, I have the sense of humor of a 21-year-old frat boy.

They NEVER send a discount code (believe me, I've checked). They send hilarious cartoons that (sometimes) feature their products. They are polarizing and don't care who they offend.

I actually slid into Karl's DMs on Instagram—which I found incredibly appropriate when considering their email content—and got on a Zoom call with him to talk about their strategy. I needed to hear it from the horse's mouth.

Karly and Karl have a Konvo:

- The birddogs team stands by their products, and they don't want to "force them down people's throats."

- They truly do write these newsletters for themselves, as it says on their site—"Jokes written for us. But you're welcome to read."
- Every week the writers come together and present a number of jokes they've come up with. The rule is that if they make everyone in the office laugh, Karl finds a way to fit them into the newsletters.

A quick, slightly off-topic story for you:

As I mentioned, I searched my inbox for a coupon. None to be found. I then went on to search the Internet, and I did find some codes. And guess what? They were BRILLIANT.

Check out the one I used:

I found a coupon for a free whistle-tip football. Somehow, I wasn't even disappointed that I wasn't saving money.

... And my husband was pumped to get a football.

To be honest, I was disappointed that the "Free Nunchucks" discount code didn't work. But hey ... you win some, you lose some.

Conversion Rate Optimization Basics

And another cameo from the CRO King himself, Dylan Ander.

Dylan and I got into a conversation about split testing, of course, and came up with a framework for email marketing.

We call it "The Big 10" –

I won't get too deep into an explanation, but at a basic level, you should be aware of the primary factors to test.

1. "The Big 10":
2. Subject Line
3. Preview Text
4. Body Copy
5. Offer
6. Design
7. CTA
8. Timing
9. Segmentation
10. Popup/Opt-in
11. Flow (Think of doing a rebrand—you wouldn't test each email individually because you need to choose one full set of emails rather than just the best performing in each test.)

Happy testing. :-)

Your Content Audit

Framework

- ☐ I am confident in the framework that is being utilized in my emails.
- ☐ I am utilizing or testing/have tested all conversion points including, but not limited to:
  - ☐ "Featured on" section
  - ☐ Social proof
  - ☐ Objection handling
  - ☐ "Contact Us" and FAQ
  - ☐ Urgency with offers

Common Issues

- ☐ I am confident my existing flow emails are optimized for mobile.
- ☐ I am confident the campaigns that have been sent out and are being sent out in the future are being optimized for mobile.
- ☐ I am utilizing best practices to mitigate issues with dark mode.
- ☐ __% of the engaged list that I send to is comprised of Outlook users.
- ☐ I am using "safe" fonts.
  OR
- ☐ I am using a fallback font with my custom font.

Conversion Rate Optimization

- ☐ I am actively optimizing my emails by testing
  - ☐ Subject Line
  - ☐ Preview Text
  - ☐ Body Copy
  - ☐ Offer
  - ☐ Design
  - ☐ CTA
  - ☐ Timing
  - ☐ Segmentation
  - ☐ Popup / Opt-in
  - ☐ Flow

CHAPTER 4

Automated Flows

Words to Know

FLOW: An automated series of steps triggered by an activity or behavior. Flows are autoresponders that can contain one or more emails and text messages and can be configured to send to contacts after a range of different tracked events occur.

UPSELL: Commonly confused with "cross-sell," an upsell is the practice of encouraging customers to purchase a comparable higher-end product than the one in question.

CROSS-SELL: The practice of encouraging customers to purchase other items that are related or complementary to their past purchase(s).

CPG: Consumer packaged goods (CPGs) is a term for merchandise that customers use up and replace on a frequent basis. Examples of consumer packaged goods include food, beverages, makeup, hair care products, etc.

EVERGREEN EMAIL: Timeless. An email that can be utilized at any time throughout the year(s) and is not dependent on a specific point in time to be relevant.

"VIEWED PRODUCT" METRIC: This metric is tracked whenever an identifiable browser views a product page on your website (for eCommerce stores). This allows you to see which product(s) your customers have viewed, when they viewed them, and how many times they viewed them.

CHURN RATE: The rate at which customers stop doing business with a company over a given period of time. Churn can also apply to the number of subscribers who cancel or fail to renew a subscription.

BNPL: An acronym for "Buy Now, Pay Later" as in the installment plans that allow your customers to pay in installments over time (i.e., Afterpay, Klarna, etc).

USER GENERATED CONTENT (UGC): User Generated Content. Any content—text, videos, images, reviews—created by people rather than brands.

VALUE MATCHING: Showcasing that a brand's values match its customers' values.

ORGANIC INFLUENCER: An influencer identified after they have already become a fan of your products. In other words, a customer turned influencer.

"Make money while you sleep."

– ~~Tai Lopez~~ Unknown

I won't get into some five page long rant about the importance of flows. You know. I know. The entire eCommerce world knows.

On average, eCom stores are generating 25% of their revenue from email marketing. We've seen brands with over 50% (no joke) from email. It's rare, but it is possible for certain brands.

But hey, 25% isn't so bad either, amiright?

One thing that I DO need to reference is the fact that email isn't just about making money. Most are only utilizing email for a fraction of its potential. The truth is that email marketing is the backbone of your customer support and retention system—it directly impacts your customers' journeys on a large scale.

This is actually where I see service providers and brands are the most short-sighted. Immediate ROI is great, but not at the expense of LTV—this is really a problem when marketers are trying to show their value on Day 1 by sending out too many campaigns to the same segment, sending out huge discounts, or sending too many discounts, etc.

Look at email marketing's potential and capabilities considering the long game.

Email marketing truly should be the core of your retention strategy. Think about building trust and loyalty. Provide value. I'll showcase many ways you can do this, whether it's via something as simple as shipping updates or something (seemingly) more complicated like organic influencer flows.

Let's start with the basics—

My team has completed more than 500 onboarding packages, the "basic" setups, for eCommerce stores over the past 4+ years. I've personally led the strategy on more than 200 of these setups.

Here's what my team, and most email marketers in general, deem as the most important flows to start with:

- Welcome
- Abandoned Cart
- Browse Abandonment
- Post Purchase
- Winback (+ Expected to Purchase aka Repeat Purchase Nurture)

And, Klaviyo's stats don't lie:

Automated Flows

These flows aren't just the foundation of your email program but the heart of your DTC retention strategy as well.

Welcome

The Welcome Flow is responsible for most of the revenue generated in the early stages of a new customer's experience with your brand.

Albeit there are always some questions about attribution, the welcome flow is important and does help capture sales, nonetheless.

You spend a lot of time and money to drive traffic to your site.

Ideally, you have a number of entry points on your site for your new visitors to opt-in. Getting these folks into your Welcome Flow can help you start a relationship with them even if they don't purchase right away.

~92% of subscribers that buy make those purchases within the first 24 hours of signing up. What about the other 8% that buy? They are going to receive the rest of your emails (welcome, browse abandonment, abandoned cart) that convince and remind them to follow through with their purchase.

To clarify, the data I am sharing in regard to purchases is from a sample of a few benchmarking stores that Segments manages. John Chao, a friend and the CEO of Tresl Segments, has graciously supplied me with this data and a few other important points I'll share throughout the book.

Here's how the welcome flow stats continue to play out:

Day 1:

- 87% of all purchases are made within the first hour
- 1% of all purchases are made between hours 1 and 2
- 3.6% of all purchases are made between hours 4 and 24

That's 91.6% within the first day!

Day 2: 1.4%

Day 3: .8%

Days 4–30: 6.2%

The Welcome Flow, aside from starting to build a new relationship and make a strong first impression, needs to convince your subscribers why they should buy NOW and why they should buy from you, all in a timely manner. As you can see from the data, the first couple of days after initial signup is crucial in turning a subscriber into a buyer.

These percentages do vary, especially when pertaining to stores with higher-priced products like furniture, jewelry, etc. To set up the most effective strategy, you should have your store's unique data on hand so you can experiment with different timing, offers, etc., to work towards increasing the conversion rates in this flow.

If you are willing to give some sort of discount in your popup/welcome, or even if you aren't, it is worthwhile to test a more aggressive approach on Day 2 or 3.

Some followup offer ideas:

More aggressive:

- Free sample, just pay S&H
- Steep discount that just covers costs (i.e., 42% off)
- BOGO

Less aggressive:

- Simple reminder of discount already offered
- Original offer + Free Shipping
- Free gift with purchase of $x+
- + many more!

Any of these and/or a change in approach in copywriting angle are good ideas to test during the first week of email sends for your Welcome Flow in the process of pushing for a sale.

And a word from the wise to small stores (or even large ones), you can also build out this flow (and/or the Post-purchase Flow) with evergreen emails—1x per week, 2x per week; whatever works with your budget and capacity—to take the place of sending some of your one-off campaigns.

Abandoned Cart

Abandoned Carts—arguably more important for immediate ROI than the Welcome Flow. Abandoned Cart Flows generally show up as one of the top revenue-generating flows for eCommerce stores.

Did you know that, on average, almost 70% of shopping carts are abandoned? Not emailing these customers is quite literally leaving money on the metaphorical table.

A quick note on a common point of confusion with the "Abandoned Cart" Flows:

There is more than one type of "Abandoned Cart" Flow.

1. Triggered by the "checkout started" metric (Traditional Version)

   a. Additional variations of this may be necessary when utilizing carts not native to your store platform.
   It's especially important to understand that you need a second variation of this flow set up when utilizing two carts at once—generally, this happens when a separate cart is used for subscriptions (i.e., ReCharge).

2. Triggered by the "added to cart" metric

What's the difference? Abandoned checkout involves abandoning the cart after the customer has entered their information in the checkout process, while "added to cart" means abandoning the cart at any stage previous to checkout.

Consider these "reasons for abandonments during checkout" from the Baymard Institute:[14]

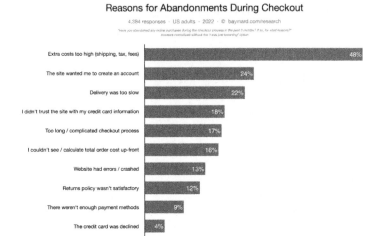

Reasons for Abandonments During Checkout
4,384 responses · US adults · 2022 · © baymard.com/research

Might any of these reasons apply to you? This data can help you craft more effective emails in this flow and may give you some insight on how to cut down on certain issues altogether. I always recommend split testing against your base so you can see the true difference a change (like adding free shipping) makes.

Here are some questions to ask yourself when considering strategy for an advanced Abandoned Cart Flow:

- Do I want to offer discounts only at a certain purchase point?
- Do I want to send different messaging based on cart size?
- Do I want to upsell another, better, and more expensive product instead of the one they have?
- Do I want to cross-sell specific products when a certain product is already in the cart?

- Do I want to create product-specific flows for the best-selling products in an attempt to improve conversions? Instead of using general language, do I tailor the messaging and pitch around a specific product or family of products?
- How many times has this person purchased?
- Will I be training people to wait for a discount with my current setup (i.e., unrestricted sends of a discount code)?
- Do I have any sitewide sales going on that would require me to update the content in these emails?
- Will I create different branches of the flow for those who have purchased versus those who haven't?
- Do I need to provide different content to people in different countries?

Design Tip:

From a conversion standpoint, I recommend nixing the "header image" in these emails. Get straight to the point. What did the customer leave behind, and why should they finish making the purchase?

Browse Abandonment

"Turning window shoppers into buyers." This flow allows you to re-engage the visitors who were browsing your products on-site but didn't add anything to their cart or make a purchase.

Browse Abandonment Flows are often one of the highest revenue-generating. Not quite as successful as the Welcome and Abandoned Cart Flows, but still essential nonetheless.

When a subscriber enters this flow, it tells you that they were on your website. And the fact that they are viewing products indicates some level of intent, but there are many reasons they may not have followed through with a purchase. Reasons may include price, speed, cost of shipping, distraction, etc.

Here are a few things to think about when crafting this flow:

- Are you segmenting by customer journey? Consider whether you may want to add in a discount or some sort of incentive for those who have never purchased (and possibly even those who have churned).
- Are you planning to send this email out to recent purchasers? If so, will you add a buffer of time where you'll filter them out? Perhaps you want to filter out new purchasers for the first two months after they buy?
- Will you exclude VIPs or regular purchasers from going through this flow entirely?
- Will you consider the number of times a potential buyer has viewed a product? Perhaps you'll take this opportunity to express urgency.

- Are there certain products you can upsell? Perhaps you don't want to push what they were looking at, and you want to showcase the better, more expensive version of the product via email.
- Do you want to create product-specific emails for your top sellers rather than send out a blanketed email regardless of what was being viewed?

Winback

Winback Flows are simple but effective. They are often discount or offer-focused because they should be triggered when your customers are close to entering the "likely to churn" timeframe in their customer journey.

Also, consider the "Expected to Purchase" aka "Repeat Customer Nurture" as an alternative or addition to this flow. A replenishment flow can also be used for a similar purpose.

How It Works

On average, it is five times more expensive to acquire a new customer than it is to retain one.[15] This flow is essential in an effort to curb churn rates amongst your buyers.

A customer will enter the Winback Flow as soon as they've made a purchase but will be filtered out if they make an additional purchase. Emails in this flow are generally not triggered for a month(s) after the last purchase, as they are intended to target churning customers.

A few quick notes on Klaviyo prerequisites for the Expected to Purchase Flow, so I don't get your hopes up:

- At least 500 customers have placed an order.
- This does not refer to Active Profiles but rather the number of people who have actually made an order with your business. If this section is on a profile but is blank, this means we don't have enough data on that individual to make a prediction.
- You have an eCommerce integration (e.g., Shopify, BigCommerce, Magento) or use our API to send placed orders.
- You have at least 180 days of order history and have orders within the last 30 days.
- You have at least some customers who have placed three or more orders.

To make this flow work, Klaviyo's AI takes a variety of data points ranging from CLV to churn risk to the average time between orders to identify the most likely next purchase dates of each individual customer.

You can utilize "predicated purchase date" triggers along with your own knowledge of your customers to build out incredibly accurate (and convincing) flows to bring your customers back for another purchase.

It's a good idea to understand your customers' buying cycle data before crafting this flow.

Some things to consider:

- What is the average timing between 1st and 2nd purchase? (Get even more segmented by looking at specific products/combinations.)
- What is the average timing between 2nd and 3rd purchase?
- Was the product most recently purchased one that you offer a subscription for?
- Are you targeting customers who are purchasing "on time" differently than those who may be considered churned or who are at risk of churning?

The Winback Flow can be as simple as an email or two sent out at your customers' average repurchase time when you're starting out, but utilizing data and running A/B tests is going to be critical to build out the most effective and personalized flows.

Assuming that you have the two week initial post-purchase built out and are sending regular campaigns, here are my recommendations for the emails in this flow:

- Build multiple forks of this flow to break up 1st- and 2nd-time buyers

1st-time buyer recommendations:

- Send out the first email at the point in time where a customer would be considered "likely to churn" and offer a discount.

- Send a reminder of the offer before the deadline ends.
- Wait 7-14 days or the time period where your customer is nearing the end of "likely to churn" and will soon be considered "churned."
- Increase the discount or change the offer. (i.e., offered 10% previously? Offer 15%, a free gift, BOGO, etc.). You can test different offers.
- Send a reminder of the offer before the deadline ends.

You can continue to build out this flow with touchpoints like occasional flash sales, etc. If someone is still in this flow and has not been pulled out, they are considered "churned," so it's time to get creative!

Post-Purchase

At a *very* minimum, the Post-purchase Flow is used to thank a new or returning customer for their purchase. This is your opportunity to continue building the relationship with your customers—get them excited about the arrival of their product(s). This flow doesn't show immediate ROI, unlike some of the others in terms of revenue, but it is incredibly valuable for long-term LTV. And, as you know, obtaining new customers is significantly more costly than retaining them.

The concept of a "post-purchase journey" is evolving as consumer demands and technology evolve. The experience provided during this time is important to building customer retention and loyalty.

Today, sending out a simple "thank you" is truly not enough. Consumers expect customized experiences that are tailored to them. They want to feel special, and they need to know that they can trust you.

Use this flow to:

- Build trust and value match
- Educate on product features, special care instructions, etc.
- Address common questions and concerns—before the customer needs to ask
- Generate excitement while the product is in transit
- Provide timely updates on shipping status—approximate arrival time, delays, delivery, etc.
- Hear your customers out—provide an opportunity to give feedback and make it easy to contact your team (ideally in real-time)
- Showcase other items they may like or that work well with what they just purchased (cross-sell)
- Gather UGC and reviews

You should look at this flow from the perspective of trying to create the most custom, seamless, pleasant, exciting experience possible for your customers. Yes, we also want to use it for selfish things like gathering UGC, reviews, and increasing LTV, but that is completely fine as long as you provide value along the way.

When done properly, this flow can help you:

- Reduce returns and refunds
- Mitigate customer services inquiries and/or issues
- Mitigate negative reviews
- Ease the adoption of and/or proper care for a product
- Increase customer satisfaction
- Increase customer LTV and loyalty
- Gather UGC
- Gather reviews
- Gather feedback on processes or product
- CREATE AN AMAZING EXPERIENCE!

I'll talk about SMS in Chapter 6, but it can be incredibly useful in conjunction with your email flow to build a seamless customer experience throughout the post-purchase process—in particular when it comes to shipping updates. If your consumers aren't already opted in, asking them to sign up to receive shipping notifications is a must.

There are many types of emails commonly utilized in this flow that can also be built out in a flow of their own or within other flows. Because strategies for these vary so widely, I'm including a short review of each below. As you read through these email ideas, consider where else you may want to utilize them.

Most common emails to include in Post-purchase Flows (or others):

- FAQ/Educational
- Subscription
- Shipping
- Replenishment Reminder and Warranty Expiring
- Cross-sell
- Upsell
- Rewards, Referrals, and Review

FAQ/Educational

Are there any common questions or product-specific instructions that can help improve your customers' experience?

Here's a great example [showing text only] from Ruggable, who utilizes this email particularly well:

My Clean Rug To-Do List

- ☐ Clean rug as needed (know your mess!).
- ☐ Remember: You can spot clean or launder.
- ☐ Be timely—clean your rug before stains settle.
- ☐ Each rug texture is different, so check:
  - ○ Chenille Rugs
  - ○ Plush Rugs
  - ○ Outdoor Rugs
  - ○ Doormats
- ☐ To store your extra Covers:
  - ○ Rug Covers: Roll or fold with design side in.
  - ○ Doormat Covers: Roll with design side out.
- ☐ More questions? Read our FAQ.

This email is awesome for a number of reasons, but here are my top three:

1. I don't have to go searching for information on how to care for my new rug.
2. I'm not going to ruin my new rug (and my experience with the company) by handling it the wrong way.
3. I'm not going to be reaching out to their customer service team with common questions because they've answered everything for me before I even think to ask.

Essentially, this email improves the customer experience, builds loyalty, and cuts down on customer service inquiries all in one!

Subscription

For the purpose of explaining how you can utilize email in conjunction with your subscription program, I'm going to reference the popular subscription app, ReCharge, and my favorite ESP, Klaviyo.

With the Klaviyo and ReCharge integration, you have the ability to trigger flows based on metrics that ReCharge pushes through:

- Subscription started on ReCharge
- Subscription canceled on ReCharge

- Order upcoming on ReCharge
- Subscription expired on ReCharge

One of my first recommendations is to create a flow utilizing the "subscription started" trigger. I use this flow to combat churn. Once you understand WHY your customers are canceling their subscriptions and gather data on that timing, you can craft emails that help mitigate churn.

For example, let's say you offer a protein powder subscription. Your biggest churn month is six months in, and you want to find a creative way to keep your buyers interested to keep them from canceling their subscription.

You decide to send them a series of emails after their initial subscription that are tailored around the primary reasons people cancel (#1 reason being an excess of protein powder).

Here's an example of how to combat this issue via email:

Last time we promised you a few recipes you can use your KOS Show Me The Greens in, so, as promised, here are three of our favorite recipes!

Greens Blend Smoothie
This breakfast smoothie is packed full of potassium, fiber, and nutrients that will fill you with morning zing—all with a fresh and fragrant taste!
[image]
Button: See Recipe

Greens Goddess Dressing

An mmm-tastic dressing with spinach, yogurt, olive oil, and avocados for a fresh, flavorful salad experience.

[image]

Button: See Recipe

Avocado N' Greens Dip

Make your next guacamole extra healthy and tasty with this delicious recipe.

[image]

Button: See Recipe

Keep in Mind: while some recipes call for specific KOS flavors, you can sometimes substitute them with other KOS goodness for new, delicious creations.

Email can be a very powerful tool to keep your customers excited and engaged throughout their subscription journey with you.

A couple other quick ideas using the basic triggers:

Canceled Subscription:

- Attempt to restart subscription (with or without a discount). You can create an entire Winback Flow off of this trigger.
- Attempt to start a gift subscription (paying for a set number of months for a friend as a gift).

- Send a survey to gather data on why the customer canceled. You can apply what you've learned to better retain subscribers in the future.

Order Upcoming:

- Upsell a one-time product to the next order.
- Last day to make changes to your order (i.e., in the case of a food subscription box where you pick your weekly meals).

Subscription Expired:

- Attempt to restart subscription.
- Attempt to start a gift subscription.
- Ask for a review or referral.

What's incredible about the ReCharge/Klaviyo integration is that you also have "Quick Action URLs" that you can utilize within flow and/or campaign emails (including the ones listed above):

- View the customer portal
- Ship next order now
- Skip next order
- Delay next order
- Add a one-time product to the next order
- Swap current subscription
- Apply discount to next order

- Reactivate canceled subscription
- Reactivate canceled subscription and apply discount code
- Reactivate canceled subscription and add one-time product

All of this shows that email can be critical to increasing LTV (and even AOV) and reducing churn in your subscription program. There are many great subscription apps out there that will have similar abilities. Understanding the capabilities of your app and the integration with your ESP is the first step!

Shipping

Order confirmation emails are a no-brainer and are generally built into merchant platforms like Shopify, but how can you make the post-purchase process seamless with shipping-related updates?

In the past, brands have been very reactive in dealing with shipping issues. Generally, even the notification of a shipping issue comes from the customer. It's time to get proactive and address the issues head-on before your customers ever have to lift a finger … not to mention that you'll win their hearts with the best automated customer service notifications on the block.

The basic notifications:

- Order Confirmed
- Shipment Created / Confirmation
- Shipment / Carrier Pickup
- Out for Delivery
- Delivered

But what else can you do to mitigate potential issues? Be proactive and build trust with:

- Attempted Delivery
- Return to Sender
- Delivery Error
- Stalled/Delay in Delivery

Thankfully we live in the world of *Wonderment* where these updates can be sent out automatically and BEFORE complaints start coming into your customer service center.

If you didn't catch that reference, Wonderment is an app that seamlessly plugs in with Klaviyo to pass through the metadata needed for personalization, segmentation, and analytics. (It allows you to send out the above emails and adds handy tags to your customers' profiles for later.)

I mention this software in particular because the "stalled/delay" metric is unique to them. You also have the ability to create "tracking pages" through their drag-and-drop builder so you can send inquiring customers back to your site instead of to the carrier's site. Hello, missed opportunity!

Example of a Wonderment tracking page:

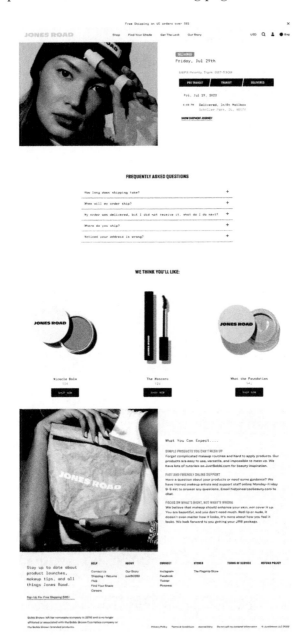

At an average rate of 20%, there are many reasons why customers return products or become frustrated with a brand—don't let a lack of shipping updates be one of those reasons.

It may sound silly, but this is the world we're living in.

My personal experience:

I ordered a pair of shoes recently (from a very large brand), and I was incredibly unimpressed with the entire process from being unable to track my package to having no idea when it would be delivered. It was my first time ordering from them, and while I LOVE my shoes, the process left a very bad taste in my mouth. It's not like the package was even "late," it was the lack of communication that bothered me. It also took a pretty long time to get delivered, which I wish I would have known would be the case. I'll probably never order from them again.

Conclusion: Today's consumers expect more in return for their business and loyalty. I mean, look at me—someone who would never even leave a bad review that is choosing not to return to a brand because of its poor customer service via lack of shipping updates.

One other thing that really could have improved my experience—an actual email address to reply to. They had a "no-reply" email address in place. A customer experience no-no!

Expert Tip:

Klaviyo now allows for emails to be triggered to send to your internal team when certain requirements are met (i.e., if there is a shipping delay, your team probably needs to know about that as well for internal operations data and/or customer service).

*Wonderment can also be integrated with the customer service platform Gorgias and Review/Rewards platforms like Loyalty Lion and even Slack.

Updates aren't the only important email types in this section. You can also send informational emails to educate your buyers where necessary.

For example, those of you who are sending products via freight may be struggling with a lack of consumer knowledge around how to receive their orders. I've seen companies in tough situations where, due to this gap in knowledge, their customers were demanding refunds on damaged products. This wouldn't be a problem if proper receipt of the packages had been made, BUT the average consumer doesn't understand the need to follow special instructions.

Here's a quick excerpt from a customer's email to give you an idea of how we helped them solve this problem:

When You Receive Your Delivery:

1. **Carefully count all the boxes in the delivery.**
   Make sure your count matches the number of boxes on the delivery receipt.

2. **Inspect all four sides and the top of each box.**
   Be sure to inspect the contents inside and out before the driver leaves. It is your right to thoroughly inspect for transportation-related damage before signing.

Inspect Thoroughly Before Signing

1. Do NOT sign the freight bill until you have carefully inspected your delivery.

2. You MUST write "Damaged" on the freight bill when signing if there is any sign of any size damage at all, externally or internally.

3. You MUST open the boxes immediately and inspect the contents (before you have signed for delivery).

4. If you discover missing or damaged items after opening the boxes, PLEASE WRITE "DAMAGED" ON THE FREIGHT SLIP WHEN SIGNING. Be as specific as possible (crushed corner, water stains, forklift damage in center of the box, etc.). WE NEED TO KNOW WITHIN 24 HOURS, OR YOU WILL NOT BE PROTECTED.

5. Contact us immediately if you find any damage.

Again, please do NOT sign the freight bill until you have carefully inspected your delivery.

Other Important Points:
1. Do NOT refuse the delivery. If you refuse the delivery, you are responsible for the cost of shipping the item back AND shipping a new item to you.
2. You MUST make clear notes when signing the Delivery Receipt/Freight Bill.
3. Take pictures of all damaged boxes from two or more angles before signing.
4. Do NOT throw away any boxes or packing materials. You may need them for return shipping.

Replenishment Reminder and Warranty Expiring

This flow is particularly important for CPG brands. Depending on product type or quantity, it's generally advantageous to send reminders when it's time to stock up again.

When reviewing timing, content, number of emails, etc., consider the quantity of product that was ordered and the time it takes to ship to your customer from the next purchase date. You'll want to send out a replenishment reminder BEFORE they run out. The goal is to get in front of the consumer BEFORE they even realize they're about to need a replenishment. This email will be that "A-HA!" moment, reminding them that they were just about to run out ... good timing! If you wait too long, you're risking the loss of a repeat purchase or, even worse, losing business to a competitor!

These emails can be utilized to push a single additional purchase and/or towards your subscription program.

You don't want to overdo it with these emails. Generally, it is a good idea to send two reminder emails and then one follow-up after the customer is considered to be churned or likely to churn that includes some incentive to complete the repurchase.

These emails can be applicable to products that are not generally considered to be CPG as well.

If you offer extended product warranties, this is a good opportunity for you to send reminders when a warranty is about to expire. Similar to this, if you sell products that must be replaced on a specific timeline in general, such as fire extinguishers, you can send out reminders to repurchase.

Cross-Sell

When people hear the word "cross-sell," they generally think about making more money from each customer. Fair—that's really in the definition, isn't it?

Cross-selling is about making more money from every customer, but, unfortunately, it's usually used in a very rudimentary way. I'll share some of those foundational insights with you, but I want to start by sharing a conversation I had with Eli Weiss of Jones Road Beauty.

Here's a little chunk of text from the transcription of our conversation on cross-selling—

"Our hero product is our Miracle Balm. It's really great for acquisition because it's unique and differentiated— there's no other brand that makes anything similar to that. The downside is that it takes roughly six months to use because it's a product that people don't necessarily need to use every day.

When we were thinking about a long-term strategy, not just what would give the fastest ROI, we thought about our replenishable products. For us, the best choice is our mascara. It's very hard for us to use that in a Facebook Ad because we're competing against hundreds of other mascara brands, but it's much easier for our customers to make the switch after they've already come to us for another product.

What we decided is that, for us, cross-selling is not necessarily about the top-selling product or even the highest profitability product. It's about the ideal customer journey for us—LTV, essentially. We know that mascara is a product that is very highly reviewed, it's used a lot, but it's not necessarily a product you'll buy first.

Let's assume it takes two or three products for somebody to love a brand, not just a product, right?

So, say someone buys the Miracle Balm and loves it, but do they love all things Jones Road? Probably not yet.

And they have probably been using the same mascara for five years, and it's not likely that this would be the first purchase, but if we can get you from Miracle Balm to a mascara and then push you into like a face pencil, that's kind of this trilogy where we know that these customers will have super high LTV.

So we really think about cross-selling in a more holistic view, instead of the typical, 'here's another way to add revenue.'"

BRAVO, Eli!

Obviously, it's very difficult for me to write generally about cross-sells ... or anything really without understanding the specifics of a brand and its products. BUT if you can look at stories like this one from Eli and think about his process rather than "cross-selling hacks," I think you'll find inspiration.

When we think about cross-sells at their foundation, we often default to thinking about bundles and added suggestions during the checkout process, but it's certainly a missed opportunity if you're not cross-selling in your emails as well. In fact, most revenue in the Post-purchase Flow usually comes from these emails.

I like to focus on the top-selling products first when creating specialized flows. Even if you add these product highlight emails in your general flow, you can set a filter to skip anyone who's already purchased a particular product. You could also start by personalizing your general post-purchase emails via displayed products utilizing Klaviyo's AI.

Do consider your profit margins here, not just those items that might work best—which ones would most benefit your company? Maybe you have a product like Eli's mascara that is the best choice for a long-term strategy.

Email marketing can be quite the investment—make sure that you're putting effort into selling the highest reward products!

And please remember that you're building a relationship. Peppering your recent buyers with cross-sell emails in your Post-purchase Flow will probably get you results, but you should sprinkle (or even pour) in real value throughout.

Upsell

How do you upsell via email, you ask? It's not an option for every store, but take advantage if you have the product fit.

These emails are generally more appropriate for brands who have multiple versions of the same product (i.e., someone abandoned their cart with a Stairclimber Pro in it, and you send them an upsell email showcasing the Stairclimber Pro Plus).

BUT it can be used in other cases as well:

- Extended or upgraded service period (in reference to subscriptions)
- Product protection addition or extension at a lower cost (warranty)
- Full product or larger sizes of a small product (often used when brands give away or sell samples)

There are also certain software, like Rebuy, that give you the ability to target customers with an upsell *even after they've made their purchase.*

Imagine being able to send an email that allows a customer to seamlessly add to their existing order if done within 24 hours of purchase—now, it's possible!

Rewards, Reviews, and Referrals

Did you know existing customers are 50% more likely to try a new product of yours as well as spend 31% more than new customers?

These stats show the importance of having a loyalty program and the makings of a good customer experience in place.

While the details of loyalty programs vary, there are some common denominators in each of them:

- How to earn points
- VIP Tiers + Special Perks
- Referral incentives

Here's Loyalty Lion's list of essential emails:

- Welcome email
- Reminder of points available email
- Points update email
- Monthly reward available emails
- Surprise and delight emails
- Seasonal emails
- Points expiry emails
- Happy Birthday

Some less-salesy examples:

- VIP-only content
- Special events (in person or online)
- Exclusive competitions to suggest or vote on a new flavor, name a new product, etc.

Some common examples of review/referral emails:

- Video request
- Review request
- Referral request
- NPS rating request

I VERY commonly see review request emails with too many barriers to entry. What I mean by this is that you can't make it a chore for someone to leave you a review—it has to be simple. Like, "wow, I don't even have to leave this email" type of simple.

Review requests are hard enough to gather—don't make it harder than it has to be.

- ✗ Linking to the site home page
- ✓ Linking directly to the product purchased <u>AND</u> to an obvious review section

Anything the customer has to do other than leave the review is a barrier. Long forms, logging into an account …

If you can remove any of these barriers, you'll very likely see your conversion rate increase.

Now, asking for a review is a no-brainer, but here are some less common emails/blocks in this category that might cause you to give me a virtual nod of approval:

For the POST Review Flows:

Good Reviews

- Thank you + leave a review on this platform as well/upgrade to a picture or video review—we'd love to feature you
- Thank you + gift card for store
- Thank you + refer a friend

Bad Review

- Customer service follow up—automated or direct outreach
- Feedback survey (the shorter, the better and higher converting)

I also recommend tagging these profiles automatically via a "bad review" profile tag in a flow. You can decide what to do with them from there, but it's important to know who these folks are.

Here's a basic example of what it looks like to combine Okendo and Klaviyo to build a Review Request flow:

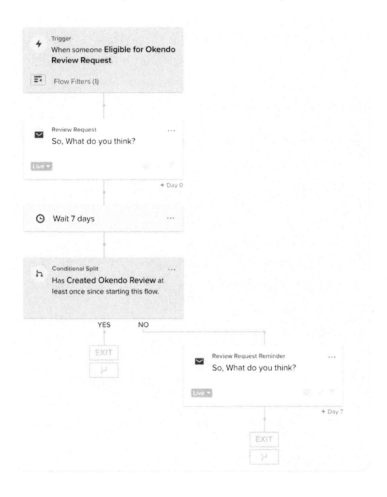

And another example of how you might use a combination of Okendo and Klaviyo after a good review to ask for a referral

Sunset

A Sunset Flow is used to remove subscribers who are no longer engaging with your brand. You can use this flow as a Hail Mary to win back their business and then suppress anyone who is not responsive. This will help you keep your list clean and prevent you from sending to unengaged subscribers that could possibly harm your deliverability.

The typical sunset setup (pre-iOS 15 rollout—summer 2021) has had a change in its filters to stay relevant, but the usefulness of the flow remains the same.

Remember that when you do set this flow up, you'll need to manually suppress those that meet the qualifications (they didn't open and/or click).

The subject line is incredibly important for this email—test a few different options. Remember, these folks aren't opening all of the other emails you sent them—that's what got them into this group of misfits. Keep the content short, sweet, and preferably plain text. Test different discounts/offers.

If you have a problem with high unsubscribe rates, you may want to use my "faux button" trick from Chapter 1.

Back in Stock

One of the easiest sales to make! You already know they're interested, and you've set up the "Back in Stock" button to ensure you let them know when they can purchase it.

The "Back in Stock" button allows you to:

- Automate restock campaigns
- Add a lead magnet for window shoppers
- Collect data on customer preferences

Here are a few ideas on ways you can utilize this flow based on your setup capabilities—

With an integration (available for Shopify and BigCommerce via Klaviyo currently):

Once you have a "Notify Me When Available" button available for each product on your site, customers can click to add the "Subscribed to back in stock" event to their profiles. Once the product(s) in question comes back in stock, this flow can automate emails to notify your customers.

This flow can be set up with general updates, including the product in question, or can be more advanced with product-specific email content.

Klaviyo or your ESP of choice will have more detailed instructions on what it looks like to set this up.

Without an integration:

Yes, back-in-stock notifications are still possible without an integration! The downside is that they are more general and not as exact, but on the bright side ... they still generate revenue.

Option 1: Send a campaign email with all recent "back in stock" items to your engaged list (limit the number of these sends).

Option 2: Send a campaign email with all recent "back in stock" items to those who viewed one of the back-in-stock products. You can do this by creating segments of folks who viewed the specific products recently.

Option 3: Send a campaign email(s) with a single "back in stock" product to those who recently viewed that product.

Option 4, 5, 6: ... you can really segment until the cows come home and even tailor these emails any way you can think of (i.e., maybe you want to angle the "back in stock" as a cross-sell email to those who purchased something that goes with it). The sky's the limit.

Birthday

Exactly what you think it is—the infamous birthday bot. If you gather DOB data, you can automatically wish your customers a happy birthday (and even a happy half-birthday) while offering a little jig (customized song lyrics), a birthday joke, or even a discount!

Once you've gathered data on your customers' DOB, you can trigger flows that send on their birthday, a day before their birthday, a week before—hell, you can count down the days to their birthday if you want to (not recommended).

Here's my half-birthday jig for you:

Go, go, go, go, go, go
Go, {{ first_name }}
It's your birthday
We gon' party like it's your birthday
We gon' sip Bacardi like it's your birthday
And you know we don't give a f**k it's not your birthday.
;)

Tip: Send birthday messages by SMS as well for a more personal touch.

Organic Influencer

Utilizing the Gatsby.ai software, collect your customers' Instagram and/or TikTok handles to identify and manage ORGANIC influencers already using your products.

It's actually pretty incredible and very simple.

Once Gatsby has your customers' social handles, it allows you to:

- Segment your customers by influence
- Auto-track when your customers @mention you in their Instagram story, post, or TikTok video
- Organize your DMs; read and respond easily
- Generate and assign Shopify coupon codes to all your influential customers/ambassadors
- Track every dollar and order driven back to your store through your micro-influencers

- Sync all insights with Klaviyo, Gorgias, and more for automated outreach, thank you's, and rewards

The coolest part for me, as an email marketer, is that all of this data from Gatsby syncs directly to Klaviyo, allowing me to build automated flows that can keep organic influencers engaged and rewarded without all of the manual work usually associated with typical "influencer" campaigns.

[end Gatsby plug]

But seriously—Brett Bernstein and the team at Gatsby have truly built something incredible. If you're doing more than 1MM in annual revenue, you are doing yourself a disservice by not scaling your community with this Gatsby app add-on

Bonus Tips

I put this recommendation together with my FAVORITE Senior Solutions Architect at Klaviyo, Mr. Andrew Smith. This man truly has such a magnificent mind, and I wouldn't want to change anything about his quote, so I'll include it here directly from the horse's mouth:

"Klaviyo can do so much more than just the out-of-the-box events that you see when integrating with an eCommerce platform such as Abandoned Cart, Started Checkout, Viewed Product, and Placed Order. In order to improve your understanding of your customer base, you can connect with more integrations, and if you have access to someone with JavaScript skills, you can track information across your site in more depth.

For examples of integrations that can be used, with Gatsby, you'll have a trigger based on someone mentioning your brand in their story. From there, you can base an event like "someone mentioned you" to trigger segmentation. You then set up automations that can respond to these triggers and even filter down on things like follower count for advanced strategies.

Another example is with Swapt, where you can have a triggered flow or segment based on a person's favorite store or promotional code they've interacted with.

For advanced marketers, an understanding based on the above examples is table stakes to have a full view of your customers, and these integrations don't require technical work.

Some advanced onsite triggers that we're seeing today that require a developer are searched site events, viewing a category, scrolling down ¾ of a page, viewing blog posts or pages outside of your store, or maybe even hovering over a Google maps area. The latter example could tell you that this person may be interested in visiting you in-store. And something like visiting in-store can even be tracked with Swapt.

The usefulness of some of these events still needs to be explored as they're not yet built to scale, but making these events today is possible with only a few lines of code.

To further clarify Swapt's capabilities—when someone scans a code or visits a location, we automate that process.

So you can say: 'Hey, let's make a segment or automation based on where someone did something or what specific promotion, either online or in person that they're interacting with.' And now, we can send them more targeted messaging, knowing more about the customer.

To sum this up, there are more ways to understand your customer base outside of what comes out of the box—custom triggers can help you do that. Whether it's considering what's happening on social platforms via apps like Gatsby, in person with something like Swapt, or having a developer capture any possible event on-site. Any of this data that you have access to should be collected and leveraged for further segmentation and automation to help you understand your full customer lifecycle."

Other common types of flows:

- Price Drop
- Wholesale Welcome, Instructions, or Updates
- Influencer Welcome, Instructions, or Updates
- Affiliate/Cross-sell Related Brand
- Purchase Anniversary

Secondary Blocks

Creating special blocks that tie in with the programs you offer can be a great use of space in your campaign and flow emails.

My top block recommendations lately:

- BNPL [Buy Now, Pay Later] Blocks
- Rewards/Referral Blocks

Buy Now, Pay Later Blocks

The use of installment plans is growing rapidly year over year.

I co-hosted a Black Friday, Cyber Monday preparation webinar last year, 2021, with John Chao, the co-founder at Tresl Segments. John's company has gathered data from more than 3,000 eCom stores over the past few years, and he had some interesting data to share regarding a study over BFCM 2020.

With the 101 different "Buy Now, Pay Later" (BNPL) payment solutions out in the market, the Segments team wondered whether customers using these payment solutions were valuable or not.

They reviewed their top-performing stores that utilize Afterpay and found that more than 10% of all revenue came from purchases paid with Afterpay during BFCM in 2020.

Breakdown of revenue by payment method during BFCM

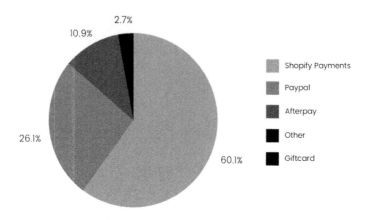

They took a look at the difference in AOV for BNPL customer versus others as well:

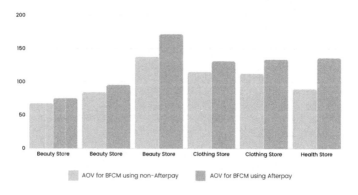

The data showed that buyers shopping with Afterpay had up to 20% higher AOV!

Then they went on to review future purchase data and customer behavior over the next 90 days (post-BFCM) versus customers who DID NOT use Afterpay.

What did they find? Afterpay customers showed a significantly higher AOV (about 48% higher average spend).

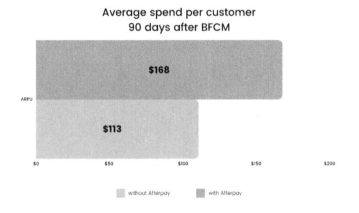

The key takeaways on BNPL from our webinar:

	With Afterpay	Without Afterpay
Average Number of Orders (ANO)	1.5	1.2
Average Order Value (AOV)	$111.16	$92.37
Average Items per Order (AIO)	2.9	2.7
Average Revenue per User (ARPU)	$167.96	$112.63

Fast forward to the spring of 2022, and John has graciously shared an update on this data with me:

"November was the highest month in terms of Afterpay orders. After 2022–01, we're still seeing growth in Afterpay orders. When comparing 2022–02 to 2022–05 versus 2022–01 orders, we're seeing increases of 7%, 25%, 11%, and 18%, respectively."

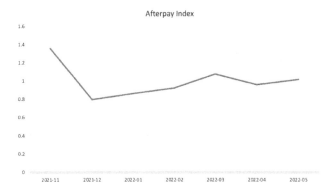

John noted that "for Afterpay, we have about seven stores in the sample. All large qualified stores over $1M+

The index is a standardized score by dividing the actual number by the mean (avg) value."

The key takeaway here is that while BNPL solutions take a percentage of your sales, they can also be a vital source of revenue for your business. Customers using BNLP options should be segmented and treated differently with targeted offers to keep them engaged and returning to your store.

BNPL blocks can be a gentle reminder of its availability, but you can also utilize campaigns and special flows to target those users (and potential users) differently.

Here's a quick example:

Here are examples of some loyalty-related conditional "blocks" for reference.

Condition = member:

Condition = non-member:

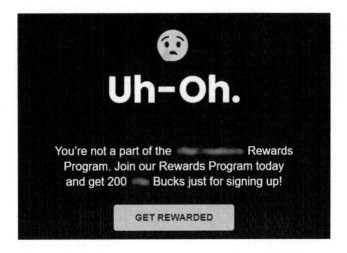

Conditional blocks can be handy in cases like this where you want to make sure any loyalty-related content is tailored for your subscribers. Here's an example of what the technical setup looks like—easy peasy:

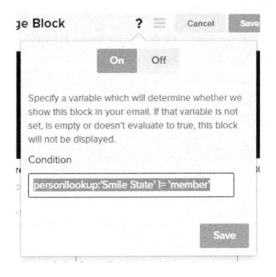

Benchmarks

Klaviyo has aggregated data across thousands of customers in different revenue bands to give you insight into areas that are performing well, as well as where you can improve.

All the tables below reference AOV (average order value).

$1-1M in Annual Revenue

Abandoned Cart Flow

AOV Min	AOV Max	Revenue per Recipient (25th Percentile)	Revenue per Recipient (75th Percentile)
$0	$28	$0.13	$0.81
$28	$37	$0.34	$1.28
$37	$44	$0.49	$1.62
$44	$83	$0.86	$2.91
$83	$112	$1.76	$5.32
$112	$163	$2.69	$8.90
$163	$291	$4.30	$13.75
$291	None	$7.77	$43.51

Post Purchase

AOV Min	AOV Max	Revenue per Recipient (25th Percentile)	Revenue per Recipient (75th Percentile)
$0	$28	$0.00	$0.16
$28	$37	$0.02	$0.20
$37	$44	$0.03	$0.27
$44	$83	$0.05	$0.44
$83	$112	$0.13	$0.97
$112	$163	$0.20	$1.39
$163	$291	$0.09	$1.92
$291	None	$0.05	$7.24

Welcome Series

AOV Min	AOV Max	Revenue per Recipient (25th Percentile)	Revenue per Recipient (75th Percentile)
$0	$28	$0.03	$0.56
$28	$37	$0.07	$1.03
$37	$44	$0.09	$1.25
$44	$83	$0.17	$1.95
$83	$112	$0.44	$3.60
$112	$163	$0.48	$5.10
$163	$291	$0.47	$6.97
$291	None	$0.32	$11.50

$1M-5M in Annual Revenue

Abandoned Cart

AOV Min	AOV Max	Revenue per Recipient (25th Percentile)	Revenue per Recipient (75th Percentile)
$0	$28	$0.20	$0.73
$28	$37	$0.30	$1.13
$37	$44	$0.71	$1.68
$44	$83	$1.12	$3.03
$83	$112	$2.39	$5.86
$112	$163	$3.86	$8.63
$163	$291	$6.00	$16.40
$291	None	$13.97	$60.48

Post Purchase

AOV Min	AOV Max	Revenue per Recipient (25th Percentile)	Revenue per Recipient (75th Percentile)
$0	$28	$0.03	$0.10
$28	$37	$0.05	$0.18
$37	$44	$0.06	$0.23
$44	$83	$0.11	$0.44
$83	$112	$0.24	$0.72
$112	$163	$0.29	$1.30
$163	$291	$0.38	$1.73
$291	None	$1.27	$7.58

Welcome Series

AOV Min	AOV Max	Revenue per Recipient (25th Percentile)	Revenue per Recipient (75th Percentile)
$0	$28	$0.03	$0.10
$28	$37	$0.05	$0.18
$37	$44	$0.06	$0.23
$44	$83	$0.11	$0.44
$83	$112	$0.24	$0.72
$112	$163	$0.29	$1.30
$163	$291	$0.38	$1.73
$291	None	$1.27	$7.58

$5M-20M in Annual Revenue

Abandoned Cart

AOV Min	AOV Max	Revenue per Recipient (25th Percentile)	Revenue per Recipient (75th Percentile)
$44	$83	$1.30	$2.88
$83	$112	$3.03	$5.07
$112	$163	$4.52	$8.13
$163	$291	$6.00	$13.58
$291	None	$15.74	$51.07

Post Purchase

AOV Min	AOV Max	Revenue per Recipient (25th Percentile)	Revenue per Recipient (75th Percentile)
$44	$83	$0.18	$0.45
$83	$112	$0.28	$0.85
$112	$163	$0.20	$1.39
$163	$291	$0.54	$2.03
$291	None	$1.01	$6.77

Welcome Series

AOV Min	AOV Max	Revenue per Recipient (25th Percentile)	Revenue per Recipient (75th Percentile)
$44	$83	$0.60	$2.19
$83	$112	$0.94	$4.55
$112	$163	$1.94	$6.23
$163	$291	$1.58	$10.40
$291	None	$1.80	$11.23

Your Flows Audit

Cross out the flows that are not applicable! Did anything in this chapter spark some ideas for you? Write them down so you can revisit them later.

Foundation

- ☐ I know how aggressive my buyers are.
  - ☐ __% of my buyers make their first purchase within 24 hours.
  - ☐ __% of my buyers make their first purchase in the first 3 days.
- ☐ I have my Welcome Flow set up.
  - ☐ I am satisfied that my Welcome Flow is optimized.
- ☐ I have my Abandoned Cart Flow set up.
  - ☐ I am satisfied that my Abandoned Cart Flow(s) is optimized.
- ☐ I have an Abandoned Cart Flow set up for my subscription software's cart, if applicable.
- ☐ I have my Browse Abandonment Flow set up.
  - ☐ I am satisfied that my Browse Abandonment Flow is optimized.
- ☐ I have my Winback Flow set up.
  - ☐ I am satisfied that my Winback Flow is optimized.
- ☐ I have my Post-purchase Flow set up.

☐ I am satisfied that my Post-purchase Flow is optimized.

☐ I have a full understanding of how each flow triggers and the filters applied on the flow and individual emails.

☐ I am comfortable with the frequency of emails being sent from campaigns and by behavior-triggered flows

Tip: Use the "smart sending" feature and profile tags to adjust customer journeys.

☐ "Time of Day" or "Day of Week" settings are implemented with a specific strategy.

These are generally more unhelpful than helpful unless used for a specific reason (i.e., sales are B2B, and emails need to be sent during working hours and between Monday and Friday).

I have these additional flows set up:

☐ Subscription Retention
☐ Replenishment Reminder and/or Warranty Expiring
☐ Sunset
☐ Back in Stock
☐ Birthday
☐ Organic Influencer
☐ Price Drop
☐ Wholesale
☐ Affiliate

I am utilizing the following types of emails in my Email Marketing program:

- ☐ FAQ/Educational
- ☐ Subscription Push
- ☐ Shipping Notifications
- ☐ Advanced Shipping Notifications (more than just the basics—"on its way" or "delivered")
- ☐ Cross-sell
- ☐ Upsell
- ☐ Rewards
- ☐ Referrals
- ☐ Ask for reviews
  - ☐ Written
  - ☐ Video
  - ☐ UGC
- ☐ Surveys

Deeper Dive

- ☐ I have reviewed my apps and their integrations with Klaviyo (or another ESP) to check for any additional data points that could help me build a more personal journey for my customers with email.

Benchmarks

- ☐ My AOV is ___.
- ☐ My annual revenue falls into this bucket: (check one)
  - ☐ $1-1M
  - ☐ $1M-5M
  - ☐ $5M-20M
  - ☐ $20M+

    *If your revenue is $20M+, please contact me for a custom performance review.
- ☐ My Abandoned Cart Flow revenue per recipient is above/below the 75th percentile (circle one).
- ☐ My Post-purchase Flow revenue per recipient is above/below the 75th percentile (circle one).
- ☐ My Welcome Flow revenue per recipient is above/below the 75th percentile (circle one).

CHAPTER 5

Campaigns

A Quick Note on Segmentation

While segmentation is utilized in triggering and filtering within flows as well, it's even more relevant when talking about campaigns.

Side note—using the word "*segmentation*" for both flows and campaigns can actually be quite confusing. Shout out to my boy Juan at Tequila Sunrise for this expert tip:

"While you can use the term *segmentation* for both campaigns and flows, I generally like to refer to the latter as 'filtering and branching' to avoid any potential misunderstanding. This is because when you are defining a particular audience—another way to say segmenting—for a specific flow, you do it by adding filters to the flow triggers and/or individual flow emails, and by adding strategic branches based on conditions."

If you're having trouble finding the right segments to target or even just having trouble building more technical segments, there is a simple solution.

Tresl Segments has been my go-to for the last couple of years. Every recent client of ours knows that this is the first app we ask them to plug in so we can build a more fruitful strategy for their initial build-out and campaign calendar.

Here are some examples of the segments you can utilize through their software:

- Churned High Value
- Churned Loyals
- Loyals
- Active Loyals
- At-Risk Loyals
- Repeats
- Churned Repeats
- Used Any Discount
- Full Price
- One-Timers
- Churned One-Timers
- At-Risk New Signups
- Low Spenders
- High Spenders
- Most Likely to Buy
- Most Likely to Churn

And these are just some of the "built-in" options; you can create any segments you'd like as long as you have the data that can be pulled in from your store platform and/or ESP. You can even sync them across multiple platforms so you're not recreating segments again.

Even if you decide not to use a special software, a sophisticated ESP can allow you to create segments that are still incredibly useful for you.

My preference has always been Tresl Segments for a few reasons:

1. Integrations—the team is adding new integrations every few weeks, and being an independent player means that if you choose to move ESPs, you don't have to start from scratch when you move.

2. Email, SMS, Ad Channels (& More)—Segments has you covered. The team has worked hard to build out integrations across not only major email and SMS platforms but also cover the major ad channels. I hear newer platforms like TikTok aren't too far off.

3. Data solidity—as Segments is a Shopify Plus certified app, its data is direct from the source (i.e., all your data from Shopify is directly piped into Segments). This means the Segments team is best placed to provide you with the most accurate segments data.

This is your sign to hop into your ESP to take a look at the options available for advanced segmentation so you can hit the right customer with the right message at the right time. ;)

Campaigns

Common Questions and Best Practices

I've collaborated with Juan Echavarria, Head of Strategy at Tequila Sunrise, to give some additional perspective on the Campaign FAQ below. He's a badass email marketer as well and always has great suggestions.

Question: How often should I be sending campaigns?

Karly's Answer: You should be sending a minimum of one campaign per week to keep your list engaged and for deliverability best practices. Outside of that, it depends primarily on whether you have the resources to hyper-target different segments of your list with variations of copy, content, design, etc. If you FORCED me to answer this question, I could generically say two emails per week, but the truth is that I'm not even comfortable with that answer, because I have no idea what your resources look like, your budget, the size of your list, your ability to create content, etc.

Juan's Answer: I agree 100% with Karly. I'd add that the engagement KPIs should always be your guide to deciding what a good cadence is. Even if you have all the capacity and resources, you shouldn't send a lot of emails if your metrics don't look right. Whenever I'm asked this question, I generally say that, as a rule of thumb, you can *slowly* increase the number of emails per week until you start getting diminishing returns on engagement metrics. For example, If you send two newsletters per week, and you see roughly the same (healthy) rates, you can consider sending a third and a fourth, etc. until you see that open and click rates start going down and unsubscribe rates start to rocket.

Of course, with advanced segmentation, you need to consider the engagement metrics of each of the audiences you are targeting and adjust the segmentation/cadence accordingly.

Q: What is the best time and day to send a campaign?

Karly: Impossible to answer! If there was a single best time and day to send a campaign that everyone used, this would no longer be the best time and day to send a campaign because everyone would be sending at that time. I know there are marketers out there that will say "Tuesday and Thursday morning" or "Mondays and Fridays after work," but the truth is that you should test different days and times for yourself. Sophisticated ESPs even have tools that can help you determine this. For Klaviyo users, check out "Smart Send Time" (not to be confused with "Smart Sending").

Juan: That's correct. And as said above, what may work as a perfect day of the week during January wouldn't necessarily work in August. Even if you find an "optimal sending time" that works well for your list, don't be afraid to retest it at least twice per year. This is a non-stop process. Something that is a general phenomenon, though, is that weekends almost always get different optimal send times from weekdays.

Q: How many sales campaigns should I send?

Karly: Again, it depends. What is your pricing strategy? Are you prepared to offer discounts on every purchase? What are your profit margins like? Are some items priced to sell while others you barely break even on? These are all important questions to ask because promotions don't need to be blanketed across your entire product line or even your entire subscriber database. You can send sales promotions every week to those who have never purchased and are considered churned. You may never want to send a single sale email to those who always purchase at full price. There are many strategies and many factors that play into a recommendation for this.

Juan: You also need to consider what we call "sale fatigue." This is when a particular brand sends so many discount codes that their subscribers no longer react to them. People no longer feel the urge to act immediately because there is nothing new about it, and codes are always available anyways. Make sure you present different kinds of sales to avoid this.

Q: What is the best way to target different segments of my list?

Karly: Are you frustrated yet with how many times I've answered, "it depends"? Well, here we go again, baby. When you think about how to do this, consider a few questions— What is my pricing strategy? How does my list break down in terms of engagement, buying habits, and behaviors? What is the long game? Is my goal to get all of my buyers onto a subscription? What is causing one-time buyers not to come back? What sort of education do I need to provide? What sort of content will my buyers (and non-buyers) appreciate? Does that answer differ by type of product they've purchased? What sort of zero- or first-party data do I have available to me regarding each subscriber I have?

I could keep going for ages with common questions and my response "It depends," but instead, I'll ask you to email me if you have any questions—karly@emailisnotdead.co— seriously, give me a shout!

Juan: You can get as granular as you want in terms of segmentation, but I'd like to stress that all potential audiences (segments) you target should have engagement components in the segmentation as a base. For example, if you want to send emails to—let's say—cat owners only, then the segment should be cat owners (preference) that have opened or clicked an email in the last x days (engagement). This, of course, wouldn't necessarily apply to re-engagement campaigns.

Benchmarks

As I shared in the deliverability chapter, your ESP should have some guidelines for you to follow in terms of benchmarks for your campaign data. There is a standard guideline that is more to help with deliverability, and then there are averages across industries that can help you compare your results to those of others in your industry.

Here are the current standard guidelines from Klaviyo:

	UNIQUE OPEN RATES	UNIQUE CLICK RATES	BOUNCE RATES	UNSUBSCRIBE RATES	SPAM RATES
Great	35% or more	2.5% or more	Less than 0.4%	Less than 0.2%	Less than 0.05%
Proficient	25-30%	1.5-2.5%	0.4-0.8%	0.2-0.3%	0.05-0.08%
Room for Improvement	20-25%	1-1.5%	0.8-1.5%	0.3-0.7%	0.08-0.15%
Critical	Less than 20%	Less than 1%	1.5% or more	0.7% or more	0.15% or more

Here are the current averages across all industries:[16]

	Open rate	Click rate	Conversion rate	Revenue per recipient
Email campaigns	31.44%	1.42%	0.09%	$0.09
All flows	50.00%	5.82%	1.64%	$1.57
Welcome email flows	50.69%	6.26%	1.94%	$1.88
Abandoned cart email flows	50.00%	7.29%	3.72%	$3.42
Browse abandonement email flows	52.85%	6.04%	0.92%	$0.88
Post-purchase email flows	58.58%	3.88%	0.40%	$0.22
SMS benchmarks	---	8.33%	0.11%	$0.09

There are also industry-specific benchmarks that you can review to get a better idea of how your email and SMS program should be performing.

Here are the current averages for Food and Beverage, one of the best-performing industries:[17]

	Open rate	Click rate	Conversion rate	Revenue per recipient
Email campaigns	32.27%	1.53%	0.20%	$0.14
All flows	51.86%	6.04%	1.93%	$1.28
Welcome email flows	53.13%	6.71%	1.96%	$1.25
Abandoned cart email flows	50.00%	7.34%	4.03%	$2.60
Browse abandonement email flows	53.33%	6.25%	1.38%	$0.95
Post-purchase email flows	59.27%	3.87%	0.53%	$0.25
SMS benchmarks	---	8.22%	0.23%	$0.16

Common Mistakes

I polled my team for a list of the most common mistakes we see brands making before they start working with us. Here are the top examples that came up:

1. Not segmenting and sending to the entire list
2. List too segmented and not engaging with as many people as they could be
3. Campaigns not frequent enough
4. Campaigns too frequent to a single segment
5. Not enough content or not a healthy balance of content between promotions
6. Too many promotions
7. Inflated open rates due to recent Apple's MPP changes mistaken as "doing a good/better job"

Questions and Ideas to Help You Brainstorm Topics

Questions:

- What types of content performed well for you in the past? Take a look through your campaign analytics to get a better understanding of what has worked and maybe what hasn't worked.
- Do you have any product launches or new arrivals coming up? If so, consider creating an entire launch strategy around it—multiple emails before, during, and after the launch.
- Can you get your subscribers involved in the business in any way? Perhaps you know you'll be coming out with a new flavor of ice cream in a few months, and you ask them to vote on the top three that you've narrowed it down to.
- Are you following your competitors or top businesses in the same industry as you? If not, follow them now and filter their emails into an "inspo" folder for later.
- Are there any products that you have high in inventory that haven't been selling well? Can you run a special promotion on them to clear out some room?
- When you break down your segments of buyers by category or product, is there a clear difference in the type of content they might like?

- What sort of zero- or first-party data do you have that could help you speak to your customers better? When you look at it, what do you see?
- What are your competitors writing about? Even if not via email, in their blog posts? On their social media pages?
- Where is there an opportunity to further educate your subscribers?

Ideas:

- Value Matching: What values does your brand hold that matches those of your subscribers?
- Blog Post Spinoff: Can you repurpose content from your blog post or other reliable blogs online that your audience would be interested in reading? You can also use email to direct your audience to new blog posts on your site.
- Seasonal: How does your product fit in with the changing of seasons? Perhaps it's the end of summer, and you have a great line of pumpkin-spice flavored treats that would be appropriate to showcase.
- Recipes: Can your product be used in a recipe? Are customers the type to be interested in them? For example, if you sell athletic wear, your customer base might be interested in "Breakfast smoothies that actually taste good."
- Ingredient or Material Spotlight
- Pain/Solution

- FAQ
- UGC Highlight
- Testimonial Highlight
- How-to
- Fun Facts
- Customer Spotlight
- Product Spotlight
- Free Shipping
- Double Points Day/Weekend
- Newsjacking

Popular holidays are a no-brainer, but what about the random why-is-this-a-holiday holidays? There are a number of them for just about every day of the year, and there are sure to be some that you can adapt your brand or products to somehow.

Here's an example of some of the "holidays" in the first few days of August:

August 1st

- Play Ball Day
- National Girlfriend Day
- National Raspberry Cream Pie Day
- Respect for Parents Day
- DOGust 1st: Universal Birthday for Shelter Dogs
- + more!

August 2nd

- National Ice Cream Sandwich Day
- National Coloring Book Day
- + more!

August 3rd

- National Grab Some Nuts Day
- National Watermelon Day
- + more!

And I bet you didn't know that August is also:

- National Peach Month
- National Panini Month
- National Hair Loss Awareness Month
- National Golf Month
- National Goat Cheese Month
- Back to School Month
- … the list, almost unbelievably, goes on.

For a full list of weird holidays, you can visit www.nationaltoday.com.

They have a list of all celebrity birthdays for you to pick and choose from. I just opened it up to June and saw that Carole Baskin's birthday is on June 6th—something to write my subscribers about.

Subject Line: "I will never financially recover from this"

And I digress …

Finally, here are some free online resources you can browse through when you feel stuck:

- www.milled.com
- www.reallygoodemails.com

Your Campaign Audit

Best Practices

☐ I am using software that builds sophisticated segments for me,
OR

☐ I have built all segments necessary for advanced segmentation within my ESP via the built-in tool.

☐ I am sending a *minimum* of 1 campaign per week (ideally more and to segmented portions of the list).

☐ I am sending to engaged segments.

☐ I have a healthy balance between content and promotional campaigns.

☐ I am using a campaign calendar and have my topics and strategy mapped out in advance.

☐ I am regularly reviewing my campaign analytics to ensure I make any necessary adjustments based on the data I see.

Benchmarks

- ☐ In general, my open rates are _____ by Klaviyo's standards (great, proficient, room for improvement, or critical).
- ☐ In general, my click rates are _____ by Klaviyo's standards (great, proficient, room for improvement, or critical).
- ☐ In general, my bounce rates are _____ by Klaviyo's standards (great, proficient, room for improvement, or critical).
- ☐ In general, my unsubscribe rates are _____ by Klaviyo's standards (great, proficient, room for improvement, or critical).
- ☐ In general, my spam rates are _____ by Klaviyo's standards (great, proficient, room for improvement, or critical).
- ☐ My campaigns have a _____ than industry average open rate (lower or higher).
- ☐ My campaigns have a _____ than industry average click rate (lower or higher).
- ☐ My campaigns have a _____ than industry average conversion rate (lower or higher).
- ☐ My campaigns have a _____ than industry average per recipient (lower or higher).

  **This number can be easily manipulated within campaigns and is not always a great benchmark to work off of.

Your Campaign Topic Ideas

Go ahead and write them down—you've got this!

CHAPTER 6

SMS + MMS

Words to Know

SHORT MESSAGE SERVICE (SMS): A standard text message with a character limit of 160. (Only 70 character limit if emojis are used.)

MULTIMEDIA MESSAGING SERVICE (MMS): A message that contains an image, GIF, video, or audio and has a character limit of 1,600.

M-COMMERCE (MOBILE COMMERCE): Mobile commerce is the buying and selling of goods and services via handheld devices such as smartphones and tablets. As a form of e-Commerce, m-Commerce enables buyers to access online shopping platforms without needing to use a desktop computer.

AGGREGATOR: A service that interfaces directly with carriers (i.e., Twilio). Aggregators act as the middleman between the carriers and the software providers like Klaviyo and Attentive.

*Note: In the U.S., aggregators are considered Tier 1 when they connect directly to the top five networks in the U.S.: **Verizon, AT&T, T-Mobile, Sprint, and U.S. Cellular**.*

THROUGHPUT: The measure of data transfer between the connections expressed in message per second (i.e., 1 message per second = 3,600 messages per hour).

S.H.A.F.T. CONTENT: S.H.A.F.T. is an acronym that stands for *Sex* (adult content), *Hate, Alcohol, Firearms,* and *Tobacco*. Note that cannabis and CBD are currently, at the time of writing this, federally illegal in the U.S. (Man, that statement is going to really date this book one day!) Vaping-related traffic is also prohibited.

**There are some strides being made in allowing CBD-related SMS, but it is currently still prohibited by most SMS providers.

LONG CODE: Generally a 10-digit, standard phone number that is used to send messages.

SHORT CODE: A short code is a 5- or 6-digit number designed for high-throughput, two-way messaging. Short codes are used to send and receive SMS and MMS messages to and from mobile phones. You'll want to be on a short code if you're sending more than a few hundred messages per day.

EXPRESS/EXPLICIT CONSENT: This type of consent occurs when someone directly tells you that they want to receive marketing messages from your brand. You can get express consent when your contact:

- Signs up via a form
- Gives you their information on an in-person mailing list (this could be in your physical store or perhaps at your booth during a conference). It's very important to retain the paperwork in these cases.
- Tells you verbally that they want to get marketing messages from you and provide you with their contact information

Essentially, the subscriber is knowingly signing up for marketing messaging.

IMPLIED CONSENT: This type of consent occurs when someone gives you their contact information but does not give permission to send marketing messages. An example of this would be someone who sends you a message on the "Contact Us" form on your website. This also, unfortunately, occurs when someone purchases something from you but does not check a box to explicitly give consent during the process. You cannot legally send SMS to these people—they must give express consent.

TCPA (TELEPHONE CONSUMER PROTECTION ACT): The telemarketing law dates back to 1991 and covers the use of automated telephone communications, including phone calls, voicemails, fax machines, and text messages. Text messages are considered transactions similar to phone calls, which is why they are covered under the TCPA. Under TCPA, sending spam text messages is illegal and can result in fines starting at $500 per infringement and reaching as high as $1,500.[18]

SPAM TEXT: TCPA defines spam text messages as any "unsolicited advertisement" that communicates the commercial availability of a product, good, or service to a person without their prior express approval or permission, whether in writing or otherwise.

CTIA (CELLULAR TELECOMMUNICATIONS INDUSTRY ASSOCIATION): The CTIA is a trade organization run by wireless companies such as AT&T, Verizon, and many more. It is not a law or government-run organization like the FCC and has no legal authority. You cannot be sued for not following CTIA guidelines; however, there can be other ramifications for not following their rules. If found to be in violation of these rules, the CTIA will report you to the mobile carriers, who may shut down or suspend your access to their customers until you resolve the issue. In addition, the CTIA established the common short code system, which is how the majority of businesses send marketing text messages to their customers and prospects. The CTIA also says any messages that contain words relating to sex, hate, alcohol, firearms, or tobacco (S.H.A.F.T.) should not be delivered.

DISCLOSURE LANGUAGE (SAMPLE): By submitting this form and signing up via text, you consent to receive marketing text messages (such as promotion codes and cart reminders) from [Company name] at the number provided, including messages sent by autodialer. Consent is not a condition of any purchase. Message and data rates may apply. Message frequency varies. You can unsubscribe at any time by replying STOP or clicking the unsubscribe link (where available) in one of our messages. View our Privacy Policy [insert privacy policy link] and Terms of Service [insert terms of service link].[19]

Writing this chapter on SMS was a BEAST.

I spent hours and hours combing through Twilio documentation (and other sources), making sense of this fairly new marketing channel. eCommerce brands have rapidly adopted the use of SMS over the last five years, but it's truly come a long way since the first "Merry Christmas" text that was sent in 1992.

My team has actually only been offering this service since January of 2020, so my hands-on experience with it has been much more limited than with email.

So, in alignment with my true overachiever fashion, I booked a flight to Boston to visit the Klaviyo team in person.

It was actually perfect timing because I somehow ended up in a room with (almost) the entire SMS team! They just so happened to be in town that week as well, and I had the pleasure of co-hosting a "fireside"-like chat along with Ted Ammon, the Director of SMS.

After all of my research and due diligence, if I had to highlight the most common mistakes I see brands making, it would rank like so:

1. Not including the proper/legal opt-in language required
2. Not including their brand name at the start of every message
3. Sending too many messages
4. Using the wrong type of phone number for the volume of emails they are sending (especially critical when starting out.)

As a follow-up to my visit and once I'd completed this chapter, Jack (from Klaviyo's SMS team) took a read-through and gave me my first piece of feedback:

Jack Binda
to me ▾

KARLY!!! WHAT A BOOK!

This is so insightful and easily digestible that you are going to help out SO many ecommerce sites with this!

And with that … I hope you enjoy this painstakingly crafted chapter on SMS/MMS. :-)

The Rise of SMS

The pandemic accelerated already existing trends toward regular online purchases, primarily CPG. To boot, new technologies and more seamless buying through systems like Apple Pay or Google Pay have continued to drive growth as well. This, in addition to new channels (including social commerce, live shopping, and influencer marketing), will also continue to spur growth.

In the U.S. alone, retail mCommerce sales grew by 41.4% in 2020 and another 15.2% in 2021 to account for ~$359 billion in sales. Annual sales are expected to double by 2025.[20]

Did you know the average American has 4 to 10 email addresses? Probably. But maybe you haven't made the obvious deduction that the majority of those folks only have a single phone number. AND did you also know that the average person spends 5 to 6 hours per day on their phone? All of this is great news for SMS marketing.

Here are some other important SMS stats to know:

Email vs. SMS Stats

	Email	SMS
Avg. Open Rate	~22%	~98%
Avg. Click Rate	~6%	~19%
Avg. Response Rate	~45%	~6%
Avg. Time to View	90 minutes	90 seconds

Another fun fact—In 2021, 71% of BFCM purchases were made from mobile devices, compared to 29% on desktops.[21]

All of this data makes utilizing SMS seem really exciting, and it is, but it isn't utilized in quite the same fashion as email. SMS and email subscribers must be treated differently. People who have opted into your SMS program are going to be much more finicky than those who've opted into your email marketing program.

Sending someone a text message is very personal, and you don't want to overdo it. It can also be very invasive and annoying. Your email subscribers might be ok with 16 emails in a month, but trust me, your SMS subscribers will not be ok with 16 texts.

Compliance

Something that isn't talked about enough in the SMS world: *compliance*.

As you read through this section, please keep in mind that many of my references are in regard to U.S. regulations and codes of conduct; laws are different in every country. And to make things more difficult, laws are based on where your recipients live, not where you are based.

In addition to that, almost unbelievably, there are literally people working around the clock to find ways to catch brands breaking compliance regulations. There have been a rise in court cases and even class-action lawsuits.

Fines currently range anywhere from $500 to $1,500 per willful violation and can add up fast.

Take a look at some of these SMS-related settlements:

- **Rack Room Shoes:** ~$26m settlement for texting their *reward program members* with various sales without their consent.
- **Papa Johns:** ~$16.5m settlement due to texting *pizza specials* to consumers without their consent.
- **Abercrombie & Fitch:** ~$10m settlement due to texting *store promotions* to consumers without their consent.

Wait for it …

Rack Room Shoes:

The plaintiff claimed that, although he gave his cellular number to Rack Room when signing up for their rewards program, he did not consent to receive text message promotions from the company.

Papa John's Case:

Papa John's opt-in agreement with SMS subscribers was to send 6 promotions per month. The lead plaintiff in this case reportedly received 7 promotions. He argued that the company was taking advantage of its customers' goodwill.

Other companies that have been on the receiving end of class action allegations in regard to TCPA (Telephone Consumer Protection Act):

- Coca-Cola
- American Eagle
- Express
- Guess
- Mercedes-Benz
- + many more!

All of this is to make a point that compliance is important and that it's only becoming more critical as SMS gains traction and is more widely utilized in marketing efforts.

Here are some of the most important things you should do to remain compliant:

- **Obtain express consent and KEEP RECORDS.** Retaining records is incredibly important. Make sure you can provide detailed records upon opt-in/out and show a record of all messages/content that was sent to each person. (Some mobile network operators require documentation on opt-ins for at least 6 years!)

- **Be transparent.** Make sure your new subscribers know exactly what they are providing their phone numbers for. This message should be displayed before people submit their phone numbers and should also include a link to your Privacy Policy page.

- **Require double opt-in.** This may look like a consumer responding "Y" to a double opt-in confirmation. This isn't a rule, but it's definitely best practice to protect yourself. Some mobile carriers actually require it if you are using SMS in your Abandoned Cart Flows.

- **Give recipients the option to unsubscribe regularly.** Carriers like T-Mobile recommend providing instructions to do so with every fifth message. Klaviyo recommends giving the option at least once per month.

- **Honor opt-outs.** Most SMS providers will suppress a profile automatically when someone unsubscribes, but it's more difficult to manage requests that may come in the form of writing (or even a phone call).

- **Only text consumers between the hours of 8 a.m. and 9 p.m.** based on their time zones. Make sure you're aware of any outliers (i.e., Florida currently has the window shortened to 8 p.m.—earlier than other states). Also, consider that an area code may not tell the full story—someone from Los Angeles could be living in New York, which further complicates things.

  *Florida also has a rule about sending more than 3 SMS in a 24-hour period in regard to the same subject matter ... do your research!

To further your use of best practices:

- **Include your brand name in every message.**
- **Provide value.** Discounts, links to helpful content, notifications relevant to a purchase, etc. SMS is much more personal and intrusive than email—the content sent via this platform should be important/relevant enough to interrupt their day and call for immediate attention.
- **Be aware of and cap the frequency of messages.** According to Klaviyo, and I agree, if you're sending individuals more than one or two texts per day, or four/five a week, you're likely sending too many and risk that person opting out.

Expert Tip:

Not sending SMS messages in the middle of the night may seem obvious, but what about the texts set up as automated flows? Ensure the platform you are using to send these messages has safety measures set to protect you from sending during "quiet hours."

By default, Klaviyo's SMS Quiet Hours are from 8 p.m. to 11 a.m. (using Eastern Time in the U.S. and Canada, BST for the UK, and Australian Eastern Time in Australia).

Regulations you should be familiar with in regard to SMS compliance in the U.S.:

- TCPA—Telephone Consumer Protection Act
- CTIA—Cellular Telecommunications Industry Association
- ADA—Americans with Disabilities Act

Here is an example of a compliant SMS opt-in form:

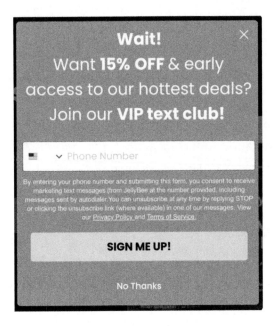

I get a lot of questions regarding express versus implied consent, so I want to stress the importance that brands understand how the CTIA qualifies types of messaging and the level of consent required.

Exhibit II: Types of Messaging Content & Associated Consent Principles[22]		
Conversational	Informational	Promotional
Conversational messaging is a back- and-forth conversation that takes place via text. If a consumer texts a business first and the business responds quickly with a single message, then it is likely conversational. If the consumer initiates the conversation and the business simply responds, then no additional permission is expected.	Informational messaging is when a consumer gives their phone number to a business and asks to be contacted in the future. Appointment reminders, welcome texts, and alerts fall into this category because the first text sent by the business fulfills the consumer's request. A consumer needs to agree to receive texts for a specific informational purpose when they give the business their mobile number.	Promotional messaging is a message sent that contains a sales or marketing promotion. Adding a call-to-action (e.g., a coupon code to an informational text) may place the message in the promotional category. Before a business sends promotional messages, the consumer should agree in writing to receive promotional texts. Businesses that already ask consumers to sign forms or submit contact information can add a field to capture the consumer's consent.
First message is only sent by a consumer

Two-way conversation

Message responds to a specific request | First message is sent by the consumer or business

One-way alert or two-way conversation

Message contains information | First message is sent by the business

One-way alert

Message promotes a brand, product, or service |
| IMPLIED CONSENT

If the consumer initiates the text message exchange and the business only responds to each consumer with relevant information, then no verbal or written permission is expected. | EXPRESS CONSENT

The consumer should give express permission before a business sends them a text message. Consumers may give permission over text, on a form, on a website, or verbally. Consumers may also give written permission. | EXPRESS WRITTEN CONSENT

The consumer should give express written permission before a business sends them a text message. Consumers may sign a form, check a box online, or otherwise provide consent to receive promotional text messages. |

Deliverability

SMS Deliverability: Whether or not a message successfully made it to your recipients' mobile devices. How does it work?

To fully understand SMS deliverability, you first need to understand the multiple layers of filters you must go through to ensure proper delivery.

The four core layers of SMS deliverability:

- **SMS Provider.** Their contract(s) with aggregator(s) are important because they outline the bandwidth/throughput allowance necessary to send messages at the time they are intended to go out. Consider a text that was sent on Monday—you wouldn't want it to arrive on Friday, would you?
- **Number.** Are you using a toll-free number? Perhaps you're using a short code? Each of these number types allots a certain throughput per second. See the chart below.
- **Carriers.** (i.e., T-Mobile, Verizon, etc.) Carriers each have their own guidelines and will filter messages based on reputation and content. Can you hear me now? Good.
- **Phone Provider.** Phone providers filter SMS messages in their own ways and are starting to evolve with the rise of SMS marketing. Android and Apple are examples of phone providers.

In short, SMS/MMS delivery amounts to reputation, speed, and compliance.

Are my messages delivered when they are supposed to be? Are they *actually* being delivered (and not blocked or filtered)?

Tips to avoid message filtering/blocking:

- Do not use public link shorteners like bitly or TinyURL.
- Include opt-out language at least 1x per month.
- The opt-out language you include in your messages must include a widely accepted keyword for opt-out. (i.e., STOP—"Reply STOP to unsubscribe.") Using other phrases like "txt 2 to opt out" is not compliant.
- Don't overuse emojis or unnecessary special characters/ capitalization, and watch your grammar and spelling.
- Monitor your opt-outs and complaints for any spikes in activity. This is an indicator that there is something that needs to be corrected. Carriers will start filtering heavily or completely block traffic as phone numbers receive complaints/high opt-out rates.

One of the fun things about carriers is that they don't always relay to you when a message has been filtered or blocked. In cases that they do relay that information, they often won't tell you the reason why. If you think your messages are being filtered, reach out to your SMS provider and/or an SMS expert for support.

Phone Number

In addition to content restrictions, you should be aware of the restrictions of the phone number you are using.

This guide from Twilio[23] explains the capabilities and key differences of long codes, short codes, and toll-free phone numbers in the U.S. and Canada:

	Long code*	Toll-free	Short code
Coverage	Can send SMS to any country	Can send SMS to any country	Can send SMS within their own country only†
Voice call capable	Yes	Yes	No
SMS filtering profile	Application-to-Person (A2P) traffic is subject to carrier filtering.‡	Verification required before sending traffic. Reduced carrier filtering to the United States, as well as the Canadian networks Rogers, Fido, Telus, and Videotron.§	No carrier filtering, as long as you adhere to the use case submitted in your short code application.
SMS throughput	1 SMS segment per second, can't be increased	3 SMS segments per second by default, but can be increased	100 SMS per second by default, but can be increased
MMS capable	Yes	Yes	Capable of MMS with a one-time enablement fee (U.S. only)

* In the United States, 10-digit long code application-to-person messaging (A2P 10DLC) will soon require business registration and be subject to additional carrier fees. Stated on Twilio site as of April 2022.

Phone Provider

Apple and Android are starting to filter new messages too. Here's a quick look at my inbox at the moment:

Messages

💬	All Messages	23	›
👤	Known Senders	9	›
👥	Unknown Senders	14	›

Did you know that this filtering system is available on iPhones *right now?* It's not the default setting, but given Apple's increased privacy push over recent years, I suspect that it could be a default setting in the future.

Android already has default versions of this folder system in use as well. In my opinion, it looks like Android is only pulling out truly scammy texts while iOS appears to be already blocking those completely and truly only quarantining "unknown" or "unengaged with" numbers without contact information.

In regard to the iOS system, as soon as a consumer interacts with an unknown number, the number then moves into their "known senders" inbox.

The truth is that I don't know how impactful this will be in the future, but I do have insight on a couple of ways that you can get OUT of the "unknown" folder in the iOS inbox should it become a problem:

- Ask customers to save your contact information in their phones by sending your contact card in the initial SMS messages. This is **not** a foolproof method, though, as very, very few people (as little as 3%) actually save the contact cards sent to them, AND it becomes very expensive to send multiple messages to every new subscriber.
- Have your customers initiate the conversation by using a two-tap mobile sign-up method or by asking them to text a phrase (i.e., "XXXXX") to your short code.

Expert Tip:

Ensure you are working with an SMS Provider that uses dedicated short codes. The industry is phasing this out, but it's still practiced. You don't want to share your short code with other brands, just as I wouldn't want a random person texting people from my personal cell phone number.

"Sending an SMS over carrier networks is like sending a postcard in the mail; they're lightweight. Sending an MMS is like shipping a package via UPS; it's a bigger file, so it's a heavier lift."

– Deanna Groshong, Klaviyo

> **Expert Tip:**
>
> Although it is tempting to send MMS messages that can sometimes have **SLIGHTLY** higher conversions than SMS, they take longer to send and require more bandwidth. If you are sending messages during a high-volume time, such as a holiday or Black Friday/Cyber Monday, it is safer to send SMS messages if you want your time-sensitive texts to arrive when they are supposed to.

Strategy

Now that you're either

1. Really excited to get started
   OR
2. Really afraid of getting sued

Let's get into some strategy basics.

Once you get through compliance and deliverability, SMS programs are actually fairly easy to manage compared to email programs. Frequency of sending is much lower, and the resources required are *very* limited. That being said, it's important to note that an SMS program should enhance your email program, not replace it.

And, getting started really doesn't have to be so scary!

SMS List Growth

First things first, are you building your SMS list? Via which methods?

Here are a few common ways brands build their SMS lists:

Via a popup, you can show to:

- **New site visitors.** My recommendation is to continue collecting email (and possibly name or other important info.) on the first step of your popup, but save SMS collection for a second stage. An increase in the number of fields to fill in on a single step generally correlates to a decrease in signups.
- **Existing customers who have not consented to receive SMS.** Use specified targeting to restrict who sees this popup.

Remember that the "Click-to-Text" option can be ideal in order to become a "Known Sender" for iOS users. This option allows your subscriber to sign up by clicking a button to send YOU a message from their phone rather than you sending them a welcome message as the first interaction.

Example of a "Click-to-Text" form:

Additional Methods:

- **Gather consent at checkout.** Certain integrations make this a seamless process by adding a simple checkbox in the checkout process.
- **Implement email banners with SMS keywords.** You can utilize this method in flows and/or campaigns. Add a mobile-only block that asks customers to sign up for your SMS program (i.e., "Text SIGNMEUP to 1 (123) 123-1234"). Don't forget to include text in the email that informs recipients what they are opting in to (disclosure language). ;)
- **Collect consent via Instagram.** Add links to signup forms in stories to swipe up. (You can collect email too.) This is currently only available to IG pages that have more than 10,000 followers.

Basic SMS Strategy

Getting started doesn't have to be complicated. Start by setting up one SMS in conjunction with each of your top-performing email flows. And, if you have an SMS list built already, send a campaign to those folks to test performance.

Welcome, Abandoned Cart, Browse Abandonment, and Winback have been found to be the top-revenue generating SMS use cases.

The top-performing SMS campaigns are:

- Sale announcements
- Holiday promotions
- New product launches

As you start to build out your program, keep your messages short and to the point, but most importantly … make them conversational and as personal as possible.

Intermediate SMS Strategy

Upgrade your program:

- Utilize zero- and first-party data to further customize your messages.
- Build 1-2 messages into each of your email flows—replenishment, birthday, VIP, etc.
- Build out your transactional messages as appropriate.

This can be particularly useful with shipping notifications.

- Segment your customers and build out a plan to send one campaign per week. Remember that each subscriber should receive no more than 2-6 per month.

Advanced SMS Strategy

Employ two-way communication.

The future of communication with subscribers is only getting more personal. This is why email and SMS (direct organic channels) are such important factors in the long-term success of an eCommerce business. These channels are unique in that they can allow you to speak directly to individuals, which isn't really possible with social media, paid ads, or marketplaces.

Sophisticated ESPs like Klaviyo will have a dashboard available where you can manage these conversations, but you can further streamline things with software like Gorgias that can pull in customer communication from all points of contact.

Benchmarks

These benchmarks are based on data from Klaviyo customers using SMS in the U.S. These ranges may vary depending on your industry and audience. (Note that rates for SMS and MMS are similar, but MMS does have slightly higher average revenue per recipient.)

SMS Campaign Benchmarks

	Click Rate	Conversion Rate	Unsubscribe Rate
Great	14.6% and above	2.1% and above	Less than 0.5%
Proficient	8.9% - 14.5%	1.0% - 2.0%	0.5% - 1.2%
Room for Improvement	6.0% - 8.8%	0.5% - 0.9%	1.3% - 2.1%
Critical	Less than 5.9%	Less than 0.5%	2.2% and above

SMS/MMS Flow Benchmarks

SMS Flow Benchmarks

	Click Rate	Conversion Rate	Unsubscribe Rate
Great	15.4% and above	3.6% and above	Less than 1.4%
Proficient	11.3% - 15.3%	2.7% - 3.5%	1.4% - 1.8%
Room for Improvement	8.1% - 11.2%	1.2% - 2.6%	1.9% - 2.5%
Critical	Less than 8.1%	Less than 1.2%	2.6% and above

MMS Flow Benchmarks

	Click Rate	Conversion Rate	Unsubscribe Rate
Great	15.0% and above	4.8% and above	Less than 1.8%
Proficient	10.9% - 14.9%	3.9% - 4.7%	1.8% - 2.2%
Room for Improvement	7.6% - 10.8%	1.9% - 3.8%	2.3% - 3.0%
Critical	Less than 7.6%	Less than 1.9%	3.1% and above

Your SMS and MMS Audit

Compliance—Consent

- [ ] My opt-in forms contain the relevant disclaimers and/or data necessary to remain compliant.
  - [ ] I have a link to my Terms and Conditions.
  - [ ] I have a link to my Privacy Policy.
  - [ ] Disclaimer includes:
    - [ ] Indication that the individual agrees to receive recurring marketing messages
    - [ ] Disclosure that messages may involve the use of an automatic telephone dialing system or "autodialer"
    - [ ] Disclosure of frequency and type of messages they will receive
    - [ ] Disclosure that consent to subscribe is not a condition of any purchase
    - [ ] Disclosure that message and data rates may apply
- [ ] I have proper compliance language wherever I allow SMS subscribers to opt-in—not just via my opt-in forms.
- [ ] I have obtained EXPRESS consent from those that I am sending SMS/MMS messages to.
  - [ ] I keep a record of consent for a minimum of 6 years.
  - [ ] I have records of the messages and content sent to each person that I send messages to.

☐ I require double opt-in when someone opts-in.

Compliance—Content

☐ I use my brand name in every message. (This is not currently required in the U.S., but it's most certainly best practice. It IS required in the UK, EU, and Australia.)

☐ I use language that provides information on how to unsubscribe at least once per month. (It's recommended to provide this with every message in countries like Canada, UK, EU, and Australia.)

☐ My messages do not contain any S.H.A.F.T. content.

Compliance—Laws and Regulations (U.S.)

☐ I am familiar with the regulations that apply to the regions where I send SMS/MMS messages.

☐ I understand that a sending compliance violation can range from $500–$1,500 per violation in the U.S.

☐ I have a process for honoring all opt-outs—even the ones that come in via phone, social media, email, etc.

☐ I only text consumers between the hours of 8 a.m. and 9 p.m. unless otherwise allowed in the regions I market to. (Sophisticated SMS providers like Klaviyo have default "quiet hours" to do this for you.)

Deliverability

☐ I am a low-volume sender and am using a *verified* toll-free number

OR

☐ I am a high-volume sender, and I am using a short code or have applied for one. (Currently only applicable in U.S., CAN, UK.)

Note that while short codes are available in both U.S. and Canada, you cannot use the same short code for both.

AND/OR

☐ I am utilizing an Alphanumeric sender ID. (Only available for sending in the UK and Australia.)

☐ I understand the concept of throughputs and how they affect my ability to send time-sensitive messages.

☐ I understand the weight/speed differences between SMS and MMS.

☐ I understand the factors that could cause my messages to be filtered or blocked.

Best Practices

☐ I am building my SMS subscriber list via multiple methods.

    ☐ I have a popup on-site for new visitors.

    ☐ I have a popup on-site for existing subscribers that haven't yet consented to SMS.

    ☐ I am gathering SMS consent at checkout.

☐ I am utilizing Instagram stories.

☐ I am utilizing SMS keywords within email.

☐ I limit sending to 2-6 messages per month.

☐ My copy is personal and conversational.

☐ I include a single, clear CTA in each message.

☐ I have built out 1-2 messages in each of my top-performing flows.

☐ I am utilizing SMS for the appropriate transactional messages.

☐ I am regularly sending 1x SMS campaign per week, per person maximum.

Benchmarks

☐ My SMS Campaign benchmarks are _____ performing by Klaviyo's scale (under or over).

    ☐ Avg. Click Rate: ____

    ☐ Avg. Conversion Rate: ____

    ☐ Avg. Unsubscribe Rate: ____

☐ My SMS Flow benchmarks are _____ performing by Klaviyo's scale.

    ☐ Avg. Click Rate: ____

    ☐ Avg. Conversion Rate: ____

    ☐ Avg. Unsubscribe Rate: ____

☐ My MMS Flow benchmarks are _____ performing by Klaviyo's scale.

    ☐ Avg. Click Rate: ____

    ☐ Avg. Conversion Rate: ____

    ☐ Avg. Unsubscribe Rate: ____

Don't Sue Me

- ☐ I have not relied upon the information in this book as legal guidance and understand I need to consult with my own legal counsel.

Recommended Tech Stack

Shopify	Merchant Platform
Klaviyo	Email Service Provider
Swapt	In-person Personalization
Wonderment	Shipping Notifications + Branded Tracking Pages
Segments	Analytics
Gatsby	Organic Influencer Management
Octane AI	Quizzes
Rebuy	Personalized Shopping
ReCharge	Subscription
Justuno	Popups
Okendo	Reviews
Loyalty Lion	Loyalty Programs
Gorgias	Customer Service
Stamped	Loyalty + Reviews
Tapcart	Mobile App Builder
Triple Whale	Attribution

Thank You

To my husband, Austin –

Thank you for being so patient with me over the past
four years. My dedication to my business and my craft
has overwhelmed our life at times, and I'll always be
grateful for your understanding and sacrifice.

To my son, Benji –

I LOVE YOU SO MUCH.

To my badass team –

There are no words to express how grateful I am to work
with such an incredible group of people. We've all
worked so hard to get to the place we are today and to
create the special culture that we have.

An extra special thanks to those who contributed to the book, whether that was through proofreading, design, change suggestions, etc.

And, of course, a big thank you to those in the industry who spent time looking through the book to give feedback and/or added additional value.

Eli Weiss – Jones Road Beauty
Dylan Ander – SplitTesting.com
Thomas Baker – Butter Pecan
Autumn Tyr-Salvia – Klaviyo
Andrew Smith – Klaviyo/Swapt
Lizzie Nirenberg Andrew – Klaviyo
Jake Cohen – Klaviyo
Allie Guertin – Klaviyo
Dan Deren – Klaviyo
Jack Binda – Klaviyo
Brett Bernstein – Gatsby
Kristina Muntean – Gorgias
Charlene Mulholland – Wonderment
Caleb Poley – Justuno
John Chao – Segments

References

1. "Every action you take is a vote for the type of person you wish to become. No single instance will transform your beliefs, but as the votes build up, so does the evidence of your new identity. This is one reason why meaningful change does not require radical change. Small habits can make a meaningful difference by providing evidence of a new identity. And if a change is meaningful, it actually is big. That's the paradox of making small improvements. Putting this all together, you can see that habits are the path to changing your identity. The most practical way to change who you are is to change what you do." – James Clear, Atomic Habits, from Ch. 2 Titled, "How Your Habits Shape Your Identity (and Vice Versa)"
2. https://www.justuno.com/blog/holiday-pop-ups/
3. https://help.klaviyo.com/hc/en-us/articles/ 4413544555547-How-to-Choose-Form-Targeting- and-Behavior-Settings#sample-behaviors---target- ing-settings-10

4. https://support.justuno.com/en/how-can-i-use-advanced-targeting-rules
5. https://help.klaviyo.com/hc/en-us/articles/360015960712#what-are-good-rates-for-a-form-8
6. https://sumo.com/stories/email-signup-benchmarks
7. https://sumo.com/stories/pop-up-statistics
8. https://www.optimonk.com/popup-statistics/
9. https://www.campaignmonitor.com/blog/email-marketing/60-exit-intent-pop-up-examples-that-convert-plus-bonus-tactics
10. https://www.drip.com/blog/popup-statistics
11. https://www.drip.com/blog/popup-statistics
12. https://popupsmart.com/help/getting-started/what-is-teaser/
13. https://help.klaviyo.com/hc/en-us/articles/360049181631-Best-Practices-for-Dark-Mode-Template-Design
14. https://baymard.com/lists/cart-abandonment-rate
15. https://www.invespcro.com/blog/customer-acquisition-retention/
16. https://www.klaviyo.com/marketing-resources/email-benchmarks-by-industry
17. https://www.klaviyo.com/marketing-resources/email-benchmarks-by-industry
18. https://help.klaviyo.com/hc/en-us/articles/360035055312-About-US-SMS-Compliance-Laws
19. https://help.klaviyo.com/hc/en-us/articles/360035056972?flash_digest=dccd84e4b-da6cb114172e07cea52a05f87ea56ab

20. https://www.emarketer.com/content/mcommerce-forecast-2021

21. https://www.shopify.com/blog/bfcm-data

22. https://api.ctia.org/wp-content/uploads/2019/07/190719-CTIA-Messaging-Principles-and-Best-Practices-FINAL.pdf

23. https://support.twilio.com/hc/en-us/articles/360038173654-Comparison-of-SMS-messaging-in-the-US-and-Canada-for-long-codes-short-codes-and-toll-free-phone-numbers